Where Are You From?: American Regions

地域で見るアメリカ

by
James M. Vardaman

TSURUMI SHOTEN

本文音声について

本書の本文音声は以下より無料でダウンロードできます。
(2020年4月1日開始予定)

http://www.otowatsurumi.com/3876/

URLはブラウザのアドレスバーに直接入力して下さい。
パソコンでのご利用をお勧めします。圧縮ファイル(zip)ですのでスマートフォンでの場合は事前に解凍アプリをご用意下さい。

はしがき

　本書はアメリカ文化を理解する重要な鍵は地域の違いを理解することにある、という視点からアメリカを11の地域に分けて説明した計11章に、アメリカを考えるのに重要な「音楽」「宗教」「連邦政府と州政府」など補足的な説明をした4章を加えたものです。

　国土面積は約9,833万平方キロメートルで日本の約26倍、人口は約3億3000万人で日本の約2.6倍、経済の規模を表すGDPは日本の約4倍の20兆5800億ドルで世界一の経済大国、これがアメリカ合衆国の基本的な姿ではあります。こうした巨大なアメリカはたとえ具体的な数字は知らなくとも誰でもが想像することができるし、調べようと思えばそうした姿はインターネットですぐ調べることができます。しかし、どの国でもそうでしょうが国土の大きさや人口、経済的な規模などを知ることは容易にできてもその国の文化を理解することはたいへん難しい。とくに国内に様ざまな文化的な違いを包含するマンモス国家アメリカを知り理解するということはそんなに単純なことではありません。

　アメリカのなかの文化的な違いを人種、宗教、世代の違いから見るのも一つの方法でしょう。しかし、冒頭でも述べたように、本書はアメリカ文化の本当に重要なことを理解する鍵は地域の違いを理解することにあるという視点から書かれました。州境は今日のアメリカを主要に区別するものではありません。説明されている11の地域の人々は、それぞれに民族的起源、言語、歴史的経験、伝統を共有しています。これらの地域は「ミニ国家」とでも呼べるのかもしれません。少なくとも、彼らはお互いにライバルの勢力圏です。彼らが使用する言葉でさえも異なるものがあります。

　本文に加えて、本書は英語自体をきちんと読めているかどうかチェックする設問を随所に設け、文法問題とリスニング問題も各章ごとにつけて総合的な英語力がつくように配慮してあります。また、各章末のディスカッションや自習用の設問は授業の活性化の一助になるように意図してつけられています。

　本書で学習する皆さんがトランプ大統領の登場以来「分裂するアメリカ」と言われることが多くなったマンモス国家アメリカが包含する地域の違いにも目を向けるとともに英語力が向上することを著者として願っています。

2019年11月

James M. Vardaman

CONTENTS

はしがき

Chapter 1　Dividing America ……………………………………… 1

Chapter 2　New England …………………………………………… 7

Chapter 3　The New York Metropolis …………………………… 13

Chapter 4　Appalachia ……………………………………………… 19

Chapter 5　The South ……………………………………………… 25

Chapter 6　American Music Roots in the South ……………… 31

Chapter 7　The Industrial North ………………………………… 37

Chapter 8　The Heartland: Prairies and Plains ……………… 43

Chapter 9　Out West ………………………………………………… 49

Chapter 10　Alaska ………………………………………………… 55

Chapter 11　The Pacific Northwest ……………………………… 61

Chapter 12　The Southwest ……………………………………… 67

Chapter 13　Hawaii ………………………………………………… 73

Chapter 14　Federal Government and States' Rights ……… 79

Chapter 15　Religion in the Regions …………………………… 84

CHAPTER 1

分割して見るアメリカ

Dividing America

アメリカへの10年ごとの流入移民数

年代	流入移民数	関連した出来事
1820	14万人	ノルウェー等
1830	60万人	原住民強制立ち退き法 (1830)
1840	170万人	ドイツ、アイルランド等。ゴールド・ラッシュ (1848–55)
1850	260万人	カトリック・アイリッシュ移民反対運動
1860	230万人	ポーランド等。ホームステッド法 (1862)
1870	280万人	南北戦争後の不況が移民流入を抑えた
1880	520万人	ドイツ移民ピーク。東欧ユダヤ人等。中国人排斥法 (1862)
1890	370万人	北・西欧の旧移民→南・東欧の新移民
1900	880万人	ロシア移民増加
1910	570万人	イタリア移民ピーク、200万人。
1920	410万人	移民割当制 (1924)。東・南欧移民制限、アジア人移民禁止
1930	53万人	大恐慌

【その後の主な動き】

1965年　移民国籍法改正：国別割当を廃止、西半球12万人、東半球17万人の上限枠を設ける。

1978年　西／東半球ごとの上限枠に代え、全体の上限を29万人に。

1990年　全移民枠を70万人とする。家族とスキル労働者を優先、未熟練労働者枠を1万人に設定。

Open Collections Program: Immigration to the Us, Timeline; Migration Policy Institute; Wikipedia 等より作成。

（ホーン川嶋瑤子著『アメリカの社会改革』ちくま新書、35頁より。）

Dividing America

Beginning with the original Native American tribes, America has been a nation of immigrants. They came in waves from different continents and migrated to available lands with different ideas of how they wanted to live, forming cultures of varied characteristics. Some factors "pushed" them out of their original homelands. Some factors "pulled" them to new homelands on the North American continent.

The early immigrants from the British Isles to the eastern shores of the country included what came to be known as White Anglo-Saxon Protestants, or WASPs. Subsequent waves of immigrants yielded competing images of "American culture" that make the WASP concept virtually meaningless in our day.

The first large wave of immigrants [1830–1860] on the Atlantic Coast were Irish, British, and German. But the second inflow [1860–1890] included these as well as Scandinavians and Chinese. The Germans were the largest participants in the third inflow [1890–1924], which was three-fourths Catholic or Jewish, with other immigrants coming from Italy, Greece, and Poland. The fourth major inflow [1945–today] included Japanese and other Asians, people from southeast Asia (Vietnam, the Hmong, Hong Kong), and Africa (Somalia, Yemen, Sudan, Congo).

●NOTES●
1 **Beginning with the original Native American tribes**「そもそものアメリカ先住民の種族たちに始まり」Native Americans とはヨーロッパの植民者のアメリカ大陸上陸以前からアメリカ大陸に住み独自の文化を築いていた諸民族をさす。／2 **came in waves**「波のように押し寄せた」／4 **"pushed" them out of ...**「…から押し出す」／5 **"pulled" them to ...**「…へ引き寄せる」／8 **yielded competing images of "American Culture"**「アメリカ文化の競い合うイメージを生みだした」移民による様ざまな文化がぶつかりあっていること。11 **Irish**「アイルランド人（語）、アイルランド人の」1840 年代からは主にアイルランドから年間 100 万単位での移民が行われたが、その契機となったのは 1845 年からアイルランドで起こったジャガイモ飢饉であった。／15– **the Hmong**「モン族」中国南部の貴州省や雲南省、タイ、ラオス、ベトナムなどの山岳地帯に住むミャオ族の支系。

Comprehension Check ▶▶▶▶▶

1. Which statement is true?
    a. American culture has not changed from the beginning of immigration.
    b. European immigrants came in four different waves.
    c. The first people who came to America were from Europe.

2. Which large group of immigrants besides those from the British Isles settled on the Atlantic Coast?
    a. Those from Asia.   b. Those from Germany.   c. Those from Southeast Asia.

🎧2 An increased inflow of immigrants into the 1920s alarmed native-born Americans who feared that the "new" immigrants would not assimilate to local ways. The native-born worried that they would lose something if too many new immigrants were allowed to come in. This has been a repeated theme throughout American history, and one that continues today. To calm the unrest, Congress in 1924 passed laws that established quotas on how many immigrants would be allowed from each country each year. This reduced the number of immigrants who were not white and northern European.

Most new immigrants entered through so-called gateway cities, such as New York, Boston, and San Francisco. They spread across the northern half of the U.S. and avoided the southern half of the country. In fact, in 1870 New York City alone had more foreign-born residents than the whole of Appalachia and the South combined.

The reasons for this are obvious. Appalachia offered few jobs, with the exception of dangerous jobs drilling tunnels through the mountains for the railroads and mining coal deep underground. In the South, land was controlled by white elites and work was done by black laborers. The Southwest was simply too remote and there were few jobs, with the exception of cattle herding.

● NOTES ●
21 **Congress in ... each year**　1924年に成立した移民法 (Immigration Laws) は、1890年の国勢調査における出身国別人口の2%の移民を毎年許可することになっていた。しかし、基準となった1890年は南欧・東欧からの移民が少なかった時代であり、実質的にはそれら「新移民」を排除してアングロ・サクソン系や西欧北欧出身者を多数とする人口構成を守ろうとしたものであった。／25 **gateway cities**: Entry point to or from a country; a primary arrival and departure point. Typically is an airport or seaport.／28 **Appalachia**「アパラチア地方」ニューヨーク州からミシシッピ州まで伸びるアメリカ合衆国東部のアパラチア山脈周辺の地域。第4章参照。

Comprehension Check ▷▷▷▷▷

3. What did native-born Americans fear early in the twentieth century?
   a. Newer immigrants would not blend into American society.
   b. Immigrants would move to the southern half of the country.
   c. Fewer immigrants from their own countries would come.

4. Which of the following is NOT true about new immigrants?
   a. They preferred to settle in the northern half of the US.
   b. They were eager to move into Appalachia.
   c. They generally entered the country through gateway cities.

🎧 3   State borderlines are not the main divisions of Americans today. It is in the regions that we find differences that help us to understand what is really important to Americans. In the following chapters, America is described as eleven regions. The people of each region believe they share a common culture, ethnic origin, language, historical experience, and traditions.

   It is tempting to call these regions "mini-nations." At the very least, they are rival power blocs. Even the words they use are different. What New Englanders call "scallions," the rest of the country calls "green onions." What the majority of New Englanders and Metropolitan New Yorkers call "sneakers," the rest of the country calls "tennis shoes." When Southerners refer to other people, they say "y'all", while the rest of the country says "you guys." A "freeway" in the western third of the country is a "highway" in the eastern two-thirds.

   The regions are based on features including topography, climate, inbound immigration patterns and periods, economic foundations, political strength, primary language, educational attainment, cost of living, social stability, and potential for attaining some version of the American Dream.

●NOTES●
42 **scallions, green onions** 日本で言う「エシャロット」の一種。／47 **topography**「地形；地勢」／47 **inbound immigration patterns and periods**「入ってくる移民のパターンと期間」

Comprehension Check ▶▶▶▶▶

5. Which of the following words are not commonly used in New England?
   a. sneakers   b. scallions   c. freeway

Structure Practice

A. Choose the one underlined word or phrase that should be corrected or rewritten. Then change it so the sentence is correct.

1. ₁<u>Almost all of</u> groups of immigrants that settle in the U.S. ₂<u>struggle over</u> how to maintain their original culture while ₃<u>adjusting to</u> a completely new culture, and this cultural conflict is commonly ₄<u>found in</u> individual families as well.

    [   ]

2. ₁<u>While</u> the early immigrants from the British Isles who settled ₂<u>in</u> the Atlantic Coast were British and Irish, later immigrants came not ₃<u>only</u> from northern Europe and southern Europe but ₄<u>also</u> from southern Europe and Asia.

    [   ]

B. Choose the word or phrase that best completes the sentence.

3. Differences between American regions .... differences in the words the people use, the foods they eat, the sports they enjoy, and the views they have about people of the other regions.

    a. include   b. consist   c. compose   d. make up

4. Competition between different immigrant groups is not .... to groups from different nations but also exists between people who came from a single country, but at different times in history.

    a. based   b. decided   c. limited   d. outlined

5. Arrivals at immigration ports on the Atlantic Coast were far more .... to remain in the urban centers of the U.S. than to attempt long journeys inland to regions where they did not have relatives or information about available jobs.

    a. advantageous   b. beneficial   c. likely   d. probable

Dividing America 5

Listening Challenge ▶▶▶▶▶

Listen and fill in the missing words.

1. One of the [   ] things new immigrants [   ] to locate was a [   ] for each [   ] of the family, even the children.

2. For decades immigrants who came by [   ] from [   ] landed at Ellis Island [   ] they were [   ] examined by [   ] agents.

3. In many [   ] immigrants [   ] [   ] working on the railroads, in construction, and in mining, jobs [   ] did not require knowledge or [   ].

4. Many new arrivals [   ] [   ] to live in neighborhoods [   ] there were a lot of people who [   ] their language.

5. Restrictions were [   ] for how many immigrants from [   ] [   ] would be [allowed] to enter the U.S. each year.

◆ Going Further (for discussion or research)

1. What are the advantages and disadvantages of immigrants coming into a country?

2. Are there any political or economic differences between American "states" and Japanese "prefectures"?

CHAPTER 2 ───────────────────────── ニューイングランド

New England

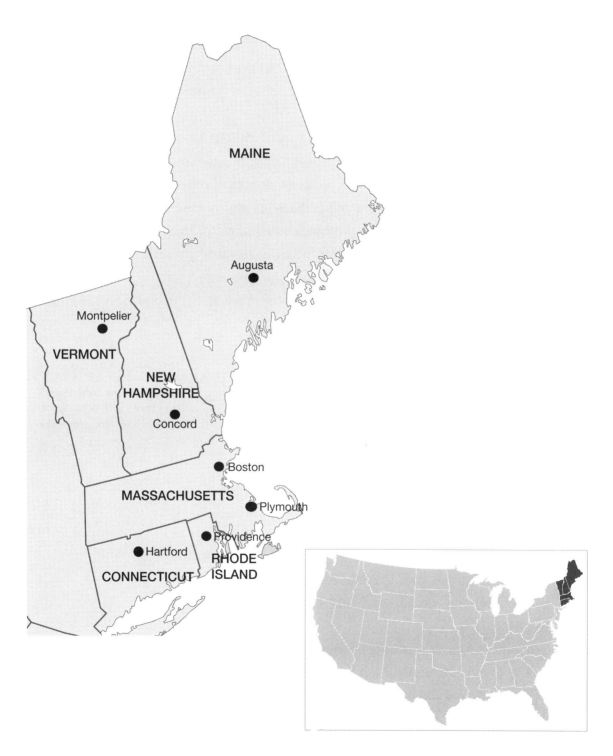

New England

Until the 1960s, almost every American child learned from school textbooks that their country was founded in New England, at Plymouth, Massachusetts, by a group of religious refugees from England known as the Pilgrims. Escaping persecution in their homeland, they fearlessly set out to establish a more open society in the New World. Every year around Thanksgiving Day, American children dressed up as either Pilgrims or Indians to celebrate the Pilgrims' legendary first harvest at Plymouth and the success of their new community. These "Pilgrim Fathers" were held to be the ancestors of the entire nation.

Such events in schools became part of America's foundation mythology that was celebrated on the fourth Thursday of November with gatherings of the members of families eating turkey, squash, sweet potatoes, dozens of other dishes, and pumpkin pie. Participants shared in a general belief that somehow or other they were recreating the first Thanksgiving feast of the Pilgrims and Indians.

This textbook-promoted foundation myth overlooked the early arrival of the French explorers, traders, and missionaries in the northern region that stretched from the St. Lawrence River to the Great Lakes and the much earlier exploration of Florida in the southeast and southwest by the Spanish.

● NOTES ●
1 **Until the 1960s**　1960年代の公民権運動等の影響を受け、アメリカ先住民族について記述する教科書もみられるようになった。／3　**persecution**「(特に宗教上の) 迫害」persecute「迫害する」／4　**the New World**「新世界」西半球、特にアメリカ大陸。the Old World「旧世界」／5　**Thanksgiving Day**「感謝祭」アメリカでは現在は11月の第4木曜日。／12　**somehow or other**「ともかくも」／14　**This textbook-promoted foundation myth**「この教科書が奨励促進する建国の神話」

Comprehension Check ▶▶▶▶▶

1. Which statement is true?
    a. Most American children have visited Plymouth, Massachusetts.
    b. The Pilgrims escaped to America for religious reasons.
    c. Thanksgiving was a tradition the Pilgrims brought from Europe.

2. What don't American school textbooks describe in detail?
    a. The foundation myth of the Pilgrims and the Thanksgiving feast.
    b. The explorers and traders along the Great Lakes.
    c. The reason why the religious refugees left England.

It was important to the Protestant colonists in New England to have printing presses to produce the Bible and other religious materials and make them available locally. The first printing publisher in colonial America was established at Cambridge, Massachusetts, in 1640. Further, the early Protestant colonists required that schools should be established in each community to teach children to read—so that they could read the Bible themselves. Their commitment to literacy placed New England at the forefront of American education, newspaper publishing, and the founding of local schools. Their "print culture" served to propagate a New England sense of moral and intellectual superiority. The New Englanders' sense of their own superiority often irritated outsiders.

The universities in New England that are included in the so-called Ivy League produce a high percent of the researchers, educators, politicians, and bureaucrats that compose the intellectual elite of the country. The cycle of success breeding success continues. Successful alumni of these universities donate major sums to the permanent endowments that fund their alma maters, keeping them ahead of universities in other states. Harvard University's endowment, for example, is currently about $40 billion.

●NOTES●
23 **literacy**「読み書きの能力：知識があること」／25 **a New England sense of moral and intellectual superiority**「ニューイングランドの道徳観や知性の優越性」／28 **Ivy League**「アイヴィーリーグ」イェール・ハーバード・プリンストン・コロンビア・ダートマス・コーネル・ペンシルベニア・ブラウンの8大学。校舎がivy（つた）でおおわれているところからの呼称。／31 **Successful alumni**「成功した同窓生たち」alumniはalumnusの複数形。

Comprehension Check ▶▶▶▶▶▶

3. The Protestant colonists in New England were enthusiastic about establishing ....
   a. farmers markets
   b. railroad lines
   c. local schools

4. The schools in the Ivy League are well-known for ....
   a. producing graduates who become members of the national elite.
   b. cultivating relationships with research institutes around the world.
   c. introducing innovative technology from their laboratories.

Today, it is the three northern rural states of Maine, Vermont, and New Hampshire that are the last bastions of Yankee spirit. In that sense, they are the remnants of New England's past. Commercial dairy farming has increased, especially in Vermont. The tourist industry has turned parts of these three states into a bed-and-breakfast heaven for tired residents of urban centers. In this sense, "heritage tourism" has become a major postindustrial "industry" in the region. State tourism bureaus currently market the region as "the authentic past," although much of that past is repainted, refurbished, and reinterpreted.

The Boston area remains somewhat apart from the rest of New England due to its concentration of academic institutions, high-tech companies, banks, and publishing companies. One feature that Boston shares with the rest of New England is its ethnic makeup. According to the *Boston Globe*, 23% of the residents of the Boston metropolitan area claimed that they were of Irish descent, the highest percentage of the top 50 most populous cities in the US, beating out other notable areas of Irish heritage like Chicago, New York, and Philadelphia. For Massachusetts as a whole, that figure was 21.5%. Italians make up 8% of the population of Boston and 13% of the population of Massachusetts.

●NOTES●
34 **rural**「田舎の、田園の」反対語は urban. ／35 **last bastions of Yankee spirit**「ヤンキー精神の最後の砦」Yankee とは本来ニュー・イングランド地方の住民をさす語。／35 **remnants**「遺物、名残り」／38 **urban centers**「都心部」／45 **makeup**「構成」／45 ***Boston Globe*** ボストンで発行されている新聞の名前。

Comprehension Check ▸▸▸▸▸

5. What most people think of as authentic New England ....
   a. is not found in the area surrounding Boston.
   b. can be found in the dairy farms of Vermont and other states.
   c. is more Irish than British in origin.

Structure Practice

A. Choose the one underlined word or phrase that should be corrected or rewritten. Then change it so the sentence is correct.

1. The ₁<u>emphasize</u> on establishing schools in ₂<u>every</u> small village with several dozen houses came from a ₃<u>belief</u> that each ₄<u>individual</u> should be able to read the Bible.
   [   ]

2. School textbooks have changed ₁<u>dramatic</u> since the 1960s, with more attention ₂<u>paid</u> to various ₃<u>minority</u> groups and the ₄<u>accomplishments</u> of women.
   [   ]

B. Choose the one word or phrase that best completes the sentence.

3. .... the Pilgrims intended to land at present-day New York, where the Hudson River empties into the Atlantic, but instead they were blown north to present-day Boston by strong winds.

   a. Fortunately   b. Ironically   c. Precisely   d. Unfortunately

4. Step by step, Boston has evolved from a British colonial town to a high-tech city in which large .... of the population are of Irish, Italian, and many other ethnic origins.

   a. areas   b. neighborhoods   c. portions   d. ranges

5. Two months from now I am scheduled to .... a report of my research at an academic meeting at another university.

   a. present   b. print   c. propagate   d. propose

Listening Challenge ▶▶▶▶▶

Listen and fill in the missing words.

1. During the [   ] many tourists [   ] through the [   ] and villages of New England to enjoy the [   ] of the trees.

2. School textbooks [   ] focus on the Pilgrims, without [   ] to the Native Americans [   ] survive their [   ] in the new country.

3. The publishing [   ] in New England but today the [   ] are based in New York City.

4. Several famous IT company founders [   ] education in Boston and then [   ] the West Coast to start up businesses that are now world famous.

5. Harvard University is [   ] the top university in the U.S., but Stanford University and the University of California [   ] in certain fields.

◆ Going Further (for discussion or research)

1. Who actually writes school textbooks?

2. What is the system for approving textbooks used in school in Japan? Is it different in America?

ニューヨークメトロポリス

The New York Metropolis

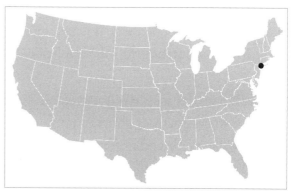

The New York Metropolis

When European immigrants sailed into New York's harbor in the 19th and 20th centuries and landed at the immigration dock on Ellis Island, they must have been overcome with anticipation, anxiety, and astonishment. Successive waves of immigrants saw an entirely different world. It remains unique, different from any other part of America. It belongs to the category of "world city" rather than that of "American city."

New York City became a major metropolis in 1898, when the five boroughs—Manhattan, Queens, Brooklyn, The Bronx, and Staten Island—were consolidated into a single city. Metropolitan New York also includes, the lower Hudson River, northern New Jersey, and southern Connecticut. The metropolis includes communities of various ethnic groups, economic levels, and cultures.

With a population of roughly 20,000,000, it is arguably the economic, commercial, financial services, media, art, theater, and fashion capital of the country. Boston competes with it in education and research. Washington, D.C., competes with it in political power. San Francisco and New Orleans compete with it as tourist destinations. But New York is the overall winner of the competition. In addition, it is an immigrant mecca; half of all immigrants to the U.S. during the past century and a half passed through New York, and many stayed there.

● NOTES ●

2 **Ellis Island**「エリス島」アッパー・ニューヨーク湾 (Upper New York Bay) の小島。もと移民局施設があった。／7 **boroughs** ニューヨーク市の行政区。アラスカ州では郡、コネチカット州などでは町。／17 **during the past century and a half**「この1世紀半の間」

Comprehension Check ▷▷▷▷▷

1. Which statement is NOT true?
    a. New York City consists of five different boroughs.
    b. A portion of Connecticut is included in the New York Metropolis.
    c. Many immigrants to America landed at Staten Island.

2. The New York metropolis can safely be referred to as ....
    a. the major focus of political power in the U.S.
    b. the main entry point for people immigrating from other countries.
    c. the most important center of education and research in the country.

Appropriately enough for a world city, Metropolitan New York offers fast food from food vendors on the streets and elegant cuisine from around the globe. New Yorkers are eager to stay ahead of the curve by sniffing out, eating at, and bragging about the newest cafés and restaurants, including places that serve Japanese food.

While Californians probably encountered sushi earlier, it was the boom in New York that made sushi popular. The sushi restaurants vary widely from places that serve hardly recognizable nigiri-zushi with "creative" ingredients to those that serve authentic fare that could be found in Tsukiji and Ginza. The more recent Japanese-related boom has been in ramen shops, each with its own recipes, prices, and diverse clientele. Matcha and other forms of green tea attract connoisseurs to shops that sell and serve tea in various forms.

The metropolis is also known for its trendy clothing fashions. In earlier years, the area known as the garment district mass-produced clothing in sweatshop conditions. Today, SOHO is filled with small shops selling clothes by low-profile fashion designers hoping to make a break into the big time.

● NOTES ●

21 **ahead of the curve**「時代を先取りして；流行の先端を行く」／21 **sniffing out**「見つけ出す；嗅ぎつける」／21 **bragging about**「自慢する；得意気に話す」／26 **fare**「食事」／28 **connoisseurs** [kànəsə́ːr]（フランス語）「目きき；つう；くろうと」／31 **mass-produced**　動詞 <mass-produce「大量生産する」／31 **sweatshop**「低賃金長時間労働の工場」いまで言うブラック。／32 **SOHO**「ソーホー地区」SOuth of HOuston／32 **low-profile**「目立たない；控えめな」／33 **the big time**「一流；トップレベル」

Comprehension Check ▷▷▷▷▷

3. The people of the metropolis ....

    a. are enthusiastic about discovering great places to eat.

    b. tend to prefer ramen to sushi.

    c. avoid trying new types of cuisine in cafes.

Irish immigrants escaping the potato famine in their own country flooded into New York in the 1850s, becoming the largest group of immigrants. In the 1880s, Italians surpassed the Irish as the dominant minority. In the twentieth century, Russians, Jews, Puerto Ricans, Chinese, Jamaicans, and others established themselves in neighborhoods where they had connections, opened groceries selling foods from the old country, and spoke their native languages. What makes New York distinctive, however, is that no single group dominates the city. Residents encounter other types of people in schools, stores, and workplaces, making New York more cosmopolitan than any other city in the United States.

One distinct area is Harlem where a distinct African American culture evolved there during the 1920s and 1930s called the Harlem Renaissance, a blooming of black music, literature, and culture. The sad fact was that blacks simply had nowhere else to go. Landlord covenants in New York kept blacks out of other areas, forcing them to settle only in Harlem, often in terrible conditions with exorbitant rents. Harlem became known as virtually one hundred percent black, dangerous, and poverty-filled. Today, the southern edge of Harlem has been "gentrified" and made safe for tourists to visit the Apollo Theater for music and to eat "soul food," an import from the South.

● NOTES ●

34 **potato famine**「ジャガイモ飢饉」1847年から51年にかけてアイルランドでジャガイモの凶作のために起こった飢饉。100万人におよぶ死者をだし、80万人から100万人の人々が主にアメリカに移民した。沈没したタイタニック号はアメリカへの移民を運ぶ客船でもあった。第1章参照。／37 **established themselves in neighborhoods**「(特定の) 地区に定着する」／44 **black**「黒人の；アメリカ黒人の」black は名詞としても用いられ、今日では Negro や nigger と違って軽蔑語ではない。／49 **gentrified**「(スラムなどを) 再開発する」／50 **soul food**「ソウルフード」アメリカ南部黒人の伝統的な料理。豚や牛の小腸やサツマイモ、トウモロコシパンなどを用いる。

Comprehension Check ▶▶▶▶▶

4. From which country did immigrants come in order to escape famine?
   a. China　　　b. Ireland　　　c. Italy

5. African American culture in the New York Metropolis ....
   a. was limited to the period known as the Harlem Renaissance.
   b. is still evident in the food and music of Harlem.
   c. has been decreasing because of high rents in the city.

Structure Practice ▶▶▶▶▶

A. Choose the one underlined word or phrase that should be corrected or rewritten. Then change it so the sentence is correct.

1. The Statue of Liberty is a ₁<u>symbolic</u> of America's openness to ₂<u>immigrants</u> from countries ₃<u>around</u> the world who are looking for a ₄<u>better</u> life.

    [   ]

2. When immigrants ₁<u>land</u> at Ellis Island, they were interviewed and ₂<u>underwent</u> medical ₃<u>examinations</u> before they were ₄<u>allowed</u> to enter the country.

    [   ]

B. Choose the one word or phrase that best completes the sentence.

3. New Yorkers are .... about discovering new restaurants and cafes.

    a. crazy   b. foolish   c. insane   d. sincere

4. It is .... to say that a majority of immigrants in the past 150 years passed through New York.

    a. fairly   b. probable   c. risk   d. safe

5. Among the recent imports from Japan that .... in New York is matcha, green tea, in different forms.

    a. hit   b. have hit   c. made a hit   d. had a hit

Listening Challenge

Listen and fill in the missing words.

1. Frederick Law Olmsted [   ] for several books he [   ] in the South, but [   ] English landscaping, he won a competition to design New York City's [   ] Central Park.

2. Greenwich Village in lower Manhattan was [   ] artists, writers, students, and intellectuals [   ] the 1960s, but as [   ] in the 1990s, it became [   ] high-income singles and families.

3. Carnegie Hall and the Lincoln Center [   ] top-class musicians from [   ] who perform classical music, jazz, and [   ] music imaginable.

4. Virtually [   ] Manhattan wants to visit Times Square to see the neon lights, [   ], watch the [   ] and buy tickets for Broadway shows.

5. Some of the best [   ] in the city are food stands on [   ], where you can [   ] hot dogs and pickles to ice cream and fresh fruit slices.

◆ Going Further (for discussion or research)

1. What would you like to see if you were able to go to New York?

2. Have you seen a movie in which New York is the setting?

3. What do you think would be different between, for example, Tokyo and New York City?

CHAPTER 4 ─────────────── アパラチア

Appalachia

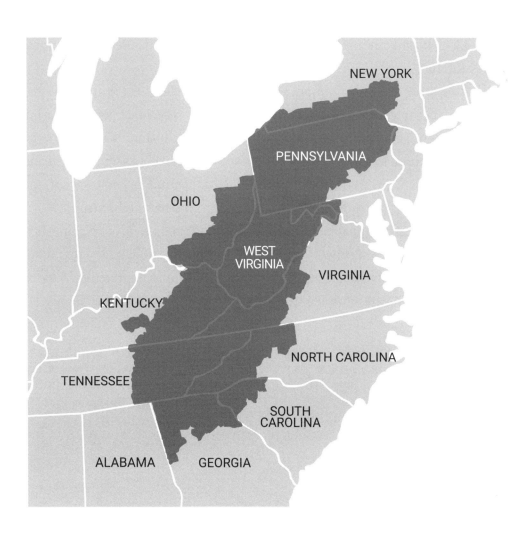

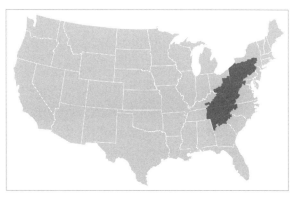

Appalachia

Appalachia has long been associated with white English speakers from Northern Ireland, poverty, low-paying jobs, low levels of education, the production of illegal whiskey called "moonshine", and fast-paced mountain music. The people who lived in this region referred to themselves as "just plain folk" but by the turn of the 20th century, outsiders began referring to them as "rednecks," "crackers," and, most frequently, "hillbillies."

Originally the term "hillbilly" simply meant a person who lives in the hills, but gradually the term became a term of contempt, suggesting a lazy white person wearing worn-out clothing who spends the day hunting and making moonshine. This stereotype of the "hillbilly" was used to ridicule the population of Appalachia as uneducated and unsophisticated. Insiders have either seen themselves as victims of industry and the federal government or as somehow inherently inferior to the rest of the world.

In reality, the people of Appalachia have traditionally been hard-working. They have had to work hard just to survive in a tough environment. Though they might not be highly educated, they have been independent; skilled at making their own tools, houses, and clothing; and careful in their dealings in the local bartering economy.

● NOTES ●
1 **be associated with …**「…を連想させる；…と関連する」／4 **just plain folk**「気取らない人；質素な人；普通の人」／4 **the turn of the 20th century**「20世紀の変わり目（初頭）」／5 **"rednecks," "crackers," "hillbillies."**「赤首」「貧乏白人」「田舎者」何れも侮蔑語。／10 **the population of Appalachia**「アパラチアの住民」ここの population は特定地域や階層の「住民」。／16 **careful in their dealings in the local bartering economy** 物物交換の損得勘定に慎重だということ。

Comprehension Check ▷▷▷▷▷▷

1. Which statement is NOT true?
    a. People who lived in Appalachia called themselves "rednecks."
    b. Residents of Appalachia have had comparatively low levels of education.
    c. Appalachia's people have felt mistreated by companies and the government.

2. Traditionally people living in Appalachia have been ....
    a. paid well for their work.
    b. skillful and independent.
    c. seen as good hunters.

The first major industry in Appalachia was timber-cutting. Then came coal mines, deep-shaft operations that by the beginning of the 20th century dominated the region's economy. Large-scale capital from outside the region established mining towns, essentially one-company towns.

Subsistence farmers gave up farming, moved their families to the towns, and became hard-working, poorly paid miners. The miners accepted whatever wages the mine companies offered, because there were no other jobs and they were afraid of losing their one source of income.

Today's mountain-top removal mining is dangerous for anyone residing anywhere nearby. This controversial technique involves scraping the topsoil off of mountains and flattening ridgetops with explosives, allowing a more economical means of extracting coal. Coal is removed, rock is dumped into valleys, and streams are poisoned by the refuse from the mines. The impact on the environment is disastrous. But local people support anyone who wants to keep the coal mines open.

Those who don't work in the mines provide a cheap source of labor for other business enterprises, in the foothills of the mountains which produce textiles, clothing, or furniture. These manufacturers prohibit unions, and workers are rarely willing to risk their jobs by protesting or organizing resistance.

● NOTES ●
18 **deep-shaft operations**「深抗操業」立抗を深く掘り下げて石炭を掘り出す操業法。／21 **Subsistence farmers**「最低限の生活の糧を得るための農業を行う農民。subsistence「生活、生存」／25 **mountain-top removal mining**「山頂を除去する採炭法」／29 **refuse**「廃棄物」／30 **keep the coal mines open**「炭鉱の操業を保つ」／34 **risk their jobs**「自分たちの職を危うくする」

Comprehension Check ▶▶▶▶▶▶

3. What was the first type of employment that changed the lives of local people?
   a. The arrival of industry in the local area.
   b. A loss of income from the sale of farm products.
   c. The expansion of the population.

4. The most recent danger is Appalachia results from ....
   a. the cutting of timber.
   b. the decline of farm prices.
   c. the new type of coal mining.

🎧 12   In Appalachia, it is impossible to produce enough on the land to even supplement another source of income. The region has the lowest average value of agricultural products sold per farm, according to the U.S. Department of Agriculture in 2012. While the U.S. average was $187,097 in that year, Appalachia was less than $10,000, an unbelievable low figure. The residents are dependent on jobs that pay a salary, no matter how hard the job may be. Unless the coal mines are hiring, people have no choice but to leave Appalachia to find work.

Outmigration from Appalachia has followed a common migrant pattern. One worker, usually a male, temporarily moves to a city outside the region, and if he finds that there are jobs, he settles there temporarily and encourages others to follow. If there are no jobs, he returns to his home. The early Appalachian outmigration spread a short distance east to the textile mills in the foothills of western North Carolina or further away to steel and factory towns like Pittsburgh, Chicago, and Detroit. The streams of migrants that flowed into the booming rubber plants of Akron, Ohio, were so large in the 1920s that this city came to be known as the "Capital of West Virginia."

●NOTES●
35 **produce enough on the land**「その土地で十分産み出す」／ 35 **supplement**　ここは動詞。

Comprehension Check ▷▷▷▷▷

5. In order to earn enough to live on, many local people ....
    a. leave the region to work in factories in cities.
    b. expand the amount of land that they farm.
    c. make hand-made furniture for sale in the mountains.

Structure Practice

A. Choose the one underlined word or phrase that should be corrected or rewritten. Then change it so the sentence is correct.

1. Appalachia is ₁ known the home of mountain music—sometimes ₂ called hillbilly music—which ₃ eventually came to be known as country music and it was originally ₄ one of the only forms of entertainment the local people could enjoy.
[   ]

2. Producing and selling whiskey ₁ without paying tax is illegal in the U.S., so ₂ to hide their production site, local people distilled their whiskey ₃ during night, so government agents could not see the smoke ₄ rising from their stills, and that's why it is called "moonshine."
[   ]

B. Choose the one word or phrase that best completes the sentence.

3. The process of cutting timber and taking it to market .... using horses to pull the timber down steep mountain slopes.

    a. consists   b. follows   c. involves   d. needs

4. Regardless of how hard the work was or how poor the pay was, workers were .... to complain, because they might lose their jobs.

    a. afraid   b. concerned   c. nervous   d. worried

5. After they .... about the disaster, many people donated money and food to help the local people.

    a. discovered   b. found out   c. realized   d. went through

Listening Challenge ▶▶▶▶▶

Listen and fill in the missing words.

1. The foothills of the Appalachian Mountains are crowded [   ] hikers and campers [   ] their busy lives in the city, but the result is often a traffic jam [   ].

2. Musicians [   ] towns on Saturdays to listen to masters [   ] group sessions, mostly playing guitars, banjos, and fiddles, and having a good time [   ] much talent they have.

3. Environmentalists protest against mining [   ] mountain tops, dig out the coal, and then [   ] to cover the gigantic holes [   ] dug.

4. People who have [   ] find that they have to drive long distances to buy groceries and to [   ], and there is no [   ] transportation.

5. The farms that remain in the hills *are more like* gardens, because [   ] small amounts of vegetables, corn, and potatoes for [   ] table.

◆ Going Further (for discussion or research)

1. Why do you think people stay in their mountain homes, even when there are no jobs nearby?

2. Would you like to live in the mountains of Japan (or another country)?

3. Which is more important—protecting the environment or having a job?

CHAPTER 　　　　　　　　　　　　　　　　　　　　　　　　　　　　南　部

The South

The South

🎧 13 The South includes the eleven states that allowed slavery until the Civil War. The "Upland South" is the northern part stretching from Virginia through northern Arkansas. Below it, stretching from South Carolina on the Atlantic to eastern Texas, is the "Deep South."

When the original Thirteen Colonies were founded, the southern colonies were different from the northern colonies. Economically, the northern colonies depended on small farms, towns, trade, and small craftworks. The southern colonies were based on agriculture, beginning with indigo and rice. The southerners began to experiment with tobacco, a crop that they learned about from the Native Americans. It was a success, and the southern colonies were the only place where such tobacco could be grown. People there began planting tobacco plants on every available patch of land because profits were enormous.

When Europe was faced with famine and lack of jobs, laborers from Europe were willing to go to the South to work. But most of the time, it was less risky to stay in Europe and struggle. The southern colonists began to import slaves from Africa to provide labor for the new plantations, which later shifted to cotton and sugar cane. This began the harsh system of slavery.

● NOTES ●
1 **the eleven states that allowed slavery** 南部の奴隷制を認めていた11州とは以下の11州である。サウスカロライナ、ミシシッピー、フロリダ、アラバマ、ジョージア、ルイジアナ、テキサス、ヴァージニア、ノースカロライナ、テネシー、アーカンソー。奴隷州であったが北部との結びつきが強く、中立策をとった州はデラウェア、メリーランド、ケンタッキー、ミズーリ、ウェストヴァージニア（1861年にヴァージニアから分離、63年に州昇格）の各州である。https://www.y-history.net/／1 **the Civil War**「南北戦争（1861–1865）」イギリス史では「ピューリタン革命」、スペイン史では「スペイン内戦」のこと。civil war「内乱、内戦」／3 **Arkansas** [ɑ́ːrkənsɔ̀ː]「アーカンソー（州）」／5 **the original Thirteen Colonies** コネティカット、サウスカロライナ、ジョージア、デラウェア、ニュージャージー、ニューハンプシャー、ニューヨーク、ノースカロライナ、バージニア、ペンシルベニア、マサチューセッツ、メリーランド、ロードアイランドの各州。／8 **indigo**「インディゴ」マメ科の植物から採る藍色染料。／14 **most of the time**「ほとんどの場合」

Comprehension Check ▶▶▶▶▶

1. Which statement is true?
    a. Native Americans learned about tobacco from the colonists.
    b. Many southerners were traders or craftspeople.
    c. Agriculture was dominant in the South.

2. The information above shows how ....
    a. the North depended on plantations and slavery.

b. cotton and sugar cane plantations depended on slaves from Africa.
   c. rice plantations yielded enormous profits.

The U.S. military has bases all around the country but the South has a disproportionate number. This is due in part to the need to train soldiers, sailors, pilots and other personnel twelve months a year. Construction of bases and large training facilities has been easier in the South because there is more open agricultural land that could be converted to military use.

The military continues to have an important impact on the society of the South and the other regions of the country. For one thing, it is a source of employment. For another, it has moved people around. Soldiers from southern states are sometimes posted outside of their home states. For many, it is the first time they have been outside the South and encountered people from other regions.

Southern blacks who went into the military during World War II and ended up in Europe often encountered a much warmer reception abroad than they had ever experienced in America. Black veterans recalled that they had been treated as Americans first and only secondly as blacks—a first-time experience for most. That kind of awakening led to determination to overthrow Jim Crow in the South and across America. When they returned to the South, many participated in the Civil Rights Movement.

●NOTES●
32 **Jim Crow** 黒人をさす蔑称。転じて南部の「人種隔離政策」。a Jim Crow law「黒人差別法」／33 **the Civil Rights Movement.**「公民権運動」とくに1950年から60年代に行われた、黒人差別撤廃を目指す非暴力的運動。

Comprehension Check ▷▷▷▷▷

3. Military bases were developed in the South ....
   a. in part because the weather was favorable throughout the year.
   b. because there were no other jobs for the people living there.
   c. in order to move the population around to new places.

4. African Americans who served in the military ....
   a. were treated well in America.
   b. later made the decision to work toward equal rights.
   c. received equal treatment in the bases in the South.

Deep South towns and cities struggled into the 1940s. It was impossible to develop large-scale factories, because machines generated heat making the factories unbearably hot. Workers could not endure more than a short period inside the buildings.

　What changed this was air conditioning. The first air-conditioning devices appeared in the 1920s in textile mills, paper mills, and bakeries. In the mid-1930s movie theaters and fancy hotels installed air-conditioning equipment to attract patrons. After World War II, however, air-conditioning became common in factories, too. Workers could stay inside and work in the lower temperatures, and heavy machinery would not break down from overheating.

　The introduction of air-conditioning changed the South in a dramatic way. It reversed a net out-migration of southerners, and initiated several phenomena collectively referred to as the Sunbelt era. First, it encouraged people from the northern Snow Belt to visit the warmer states as tourists. Second, it brought new industries and businesses to the South, where land was less expensive. Third, it promoted the urbanization of the South, accelerating population growth through high-rise buildings for business and residences, especially appealing to retirees from the Snow Belt. In addition, five of the most tax-friendly states for retirees are in the South.

●NOTES●
35 **struggled into the 1940s**「1940年代を苦労してやっていった」／46 **a net out-migration**「純移出数」out-migrationとは、産業な盛んな地方で働くために人が大規模に移出すること。反対語は in-migration。／46 **several phenomena collectively referred to as …**「…と総称して呼ぶいくつかの現象」phenomena<phenomenon／47 **the Sunbelt era**「サンベルト時代」Sunbeltはカリフォルニア州からヴァージニア州に至る温暖地帯のこと。／47 **the northern Snow Belt**「北部スノウベルト」大西洋からロッキー山脈北部に至る北部地帯。／52 **tax-friendly states for retirees**「退職生活者に税金が好意的な州」

Comprehension Check ▷▷▷▷▷

5. When air-conditioning became available, ...
    a. it was first introduced in ordinary homes.
    b. it had no impact on tourism in the southern states.
    c. it was first installed in factories to reduce the heat caused by machinery.

Structure Practice

A. Choose the one underlined word or phrase that should be corrected or rewritten. Then change it so the sentence is correct.

1. The <u>₁economy</u> in the small town in Mississippi where I <u>₂grew</u> up was based <u>₃in</u> timber, pulp wood <u>₄for</u> paper, and the production of turpentine.
    [   ]

2. The warmer southern states are not <u>₁suitable</u> for wheat or for <u>₂raising</u> cows and horses but they are the only <u>₃place</u> in the U.S. where cotton <u>₄grow</u>.
    [   ]

3. Since she <u>₁needed</u> to <u>₂increase</u> production, the manager decided to <u>₃insert</u> two <u>₄additional</u> printing machines.   [   ]

B. Choose the one word or phrase that best completes the sentence.

4. When there were enough jobs in Europe, most laborers felt it was .... to take a chance on crossing the Atlantic to work in the colonies.

    a. risk   b. risked   c. risking   d. risky

5. The Europeans' desire to purchase tobacco .... the colonists in the South to grow as much as possible.

    a. impacted   b. affected   c. effected   d. influenced

Listening Challenge

Listen and fill in the missing words.

1. People in the South [   ] of both football and basketball, but the [   ] so popular that the highest paid [   ] in most southern states is not the governor or [   ] but a university football team coach.

2. Kentucky [   ] bourbon whiskey, which is produced in Bourbon County, a small area [   ] of the state, where [   ] making that type of alcoholic drink.

3. Not everyone [   ] but most southerners [   ] of deep-fried food, [   ] and fried catfish, both of which are [   ] health foods.

4. African Americans have [   ] to every aspect of American life and [   ] century have more Americans [   ] that.

5. The humidity and [   ] in the Deep South is [   ] as those of Tokyo [   ] July and August.

◆ Going Further (for discussion or research)

1. What do you know about the Civil Rights Movement in the 1950s and 1960s in the U.S.?

2. Do you think that relations between blacks and whites in the South are better today?

3. Where are the headquarters of Coca-Cola and CNN?

CHAPTER

南部のアメリカ音楽のルーツ

American Music Roots in the South

American Music Roots in the South

American music has many roots in the South. White Europeans who settled in the South brought traditional folk music and religious music. They adapted traditional folk songs using American stories and lyrics. They combined the old with the new and created mountain music, later called hillbilly music and then country music, to entertain themselves and forget about their harsh living conditions.

Enslaved Africans used instruments they were familiar with, including drums and simple stringed instruments. They added lyrics about the cruel treatment they received from slave masters and harsh working conditions in the fields and created music called the blues. They heard stories from the Bible and English songs in churches and made their own sacred songs, called spirituals.

After the Civil War, some former slaves moved to New Orleans and used their unique blues sounds to earn money or just to have a good time. When blacks and creoles of color played together, they mixed the free sounds and blue notes of blues with European band and orchestra music and created a hot new sound called jazz. That music went up the Mississippi River to St. Louis, to Chicago, and then to New York. It became popular around the world. The roots, however, were all in the South.

● NOTES ●

4 **hillbilly music**「アパラチアの音楽」4章を参照のこと。／13 **creoles of color** ルイジアナの旧フランスとスペインの植民地（特にニューオーリンズの街）、ミシシッピ州南部、アラバマ州、フロリダ州北西部で発達したクレオール人の歴史的な民族グループ。クレオール人とは植民地で生まれたネイティブ以外の人々を言う。／13 **blue notes of blues** ブルースの旋律に表れる音階的な特徴。note「音、音色；音符」

Comprehension Check ▶▶▶▶▶

1. Which statement is true?
    a. White southerners continued European music without changing it.
    b. Enslaved Africans adapted European music from the churches.
    c. Jazz developed in the North among white musicians.

2. The unique sounds of jazz music ....
    a. reached New Orleans from Chicago and New York.
    b. originated in mountain music and spirituals.
    c. were created by creoles and black southerners.

During slavery, black southerners kept the spirituals they created secret. They did not want white people to hear the music that came from their hearts. After slavery was abolished, however, groups of students at Fisk College, a black college in Nashville, traveled in the North singing European choral music to raise money for their school. On one occasion, they sang an old spiritual for the first time in public. White audiences were greatly moved by it, and spirituals became a new American genre.

By the end of the 19th century, black musicians no longer wanted to sing the songs of the days of slavery. When blues and jazz became popular, creative musicians changed spirituals into a commercial sacred music called gospel. Black gospel choirs and white gospel choirs developed into separate branches, but from the same roots.

Black and white southern musicians listened to one another and developed other genres of music. Bill Monroe, a white musician who played stringed-based mountain music added blues sounds to create fast-paced music called bluegrass. Muddy Waters, a black musician from Mississippi who played country blues moved to Chicago, began experimenting with an electric guitar and created urban blues for city people.

● NOTES ●
17 **spirituals** 複数形で「黒人霊歌；教会関係の事柄」／20 **raise money for ...**「…のための金を調達する」／21 **On one occasion**「あるとき」／28 **Bill Monroe** 1911–96。／29 **bluegrass** ギター・バンジョー・フィドルなどで演奏されるテンポの速いカントリーミュージック。／29 **Muddy Waters** 1913–83。

Comprehension Check ▷▷▷▷▷

3. Which statement is NOT true?
   a. Southern whites heard spirituals before the Civil War.
   b. Spirituals lost popularity and gospel music became more popular.
   c. The first group to make spirituals known to the white public were from Fisk College.

4. How did southern music change?
   a. Black musicians took over the lyrics of mountain music.
   b. Country blues evolved into blues for city people.
   c. Country blues musicians borrowed from black gospel singers.

🎧 18 Elvis Presley, a young white truck driver in Memphis, listened to all kinds of music on local radio stations. Building on all of the roots of Southern music—blues, gospel, bluegrass, and country music—he created a new sound that came to be called rock and roll. He was not the only creator and he always gave credit to black and white musicians he borrowed from. But he made it into something that no one had heard before. It spread across the U.S., and, of course, around the world. There would be no Beatles without it.

In the 1920s, religious music that was born in churches came to be performed outside the churches as well. This new music was called gospel and it became a widely appreciated genre thanks to performers like Mahalia Jackson on television. It appealed to audiences of all colors. Following Mahalia, another singer with roots deep in Southern church gospel took religious music in another direction. This singer was the daughter of a well-known black minister and she cultivated her talent in black churches. Her name was Aretha Franklin. While keeping one foot in church music, Aretha developed a new genre called soul music. At first some church members disliked it, but very quickly Aretha's music became famous around the world.

●NOTES●
32 **Elvis Presley** 1935–77。／32 **Memphis** メンフィスはテネシー州南西部のミシシッピ川に臨む市。／35 **He was not the only creator**「彼が自分だけで創り出したのではなかった」／35 **gave credit to ...**「…を評価する、功績を認める」／40 **became a widely appreciated genre**「広く認められるジャンルとなった」／41 **Mahalia Jackson** 1911–72。／45 **Aretha Franklin** 1942–2018。メンフィスの生まれ。パワフルな女性像、女性解放運動、公民権運動を象徴する存在となった。Lady Soul、Queen of Soul と呼ばれる。

Comprehension Check ▷▷▷▷▷▷

5. How were Elvis Presley and Aretha Franklin different?
    a. Only one borrowed from church music.
    b. Only one borrowed from bluegrass music.
    c. Only one of them became famous.

Structure Practice ▶▶▶▶▶

A. Choose the one underlined word or phrase that should be corrected or rewritten. Then change it so the sentence is correct.

1. Musicians who play ₁ one variety of roots music ₂ almost invariably found ₃ another type of music they were ₄ interested. [   ]

2. Southern music has ₁ deep roots not ₂ only in the churches but also ₃ in the traditional music forms ₄ originate in Africa and Europe. [   ]

B. Choose the one word or phrase that best completes the sentence.

3. A song that enslaved black people sang among themselves is called a ....
   a. church song   b. religious music   c. spiritual   d. gospel

4. .... blues and orchestral music that came from Europe, jazz musicians developed an entirely new sound.
   a. Blending   b. Creating   c. Evolving   d. Excepting

5. Around the world .... were impressed by the music created by both Aretha and Elvis.
   a. genres   b. viewers   c. spectators   d. audiences

Listening Challenge ▶▶▶▶▶

Listen and fill in the missing words.

1. It is [   ] the world was excited by The Beatles when they performed and issued new albums, but [   ] that they were stimulated by musicians from the South.

2. In order to perform orchestral music, [   ] read sheet music and [   ] a conductor.

3. What classical musicians [   ] violin [   ] a fiddle in country music.

4. Country blues musicians in the South played [   ] juke joints where people came [   ] how harsh their work lives were.

5. New Orleans was [   ] in the U.S. where well-trained orchestra musicians and creative blues musicians [   ] one another.

◆ Going Further (for discussion or research)

1. Can you name any famous Japanese or American jazz musicians?

2. In what ways is music appealing to people?

CHAPTER 7 ── 工業の北部

The Industrial North

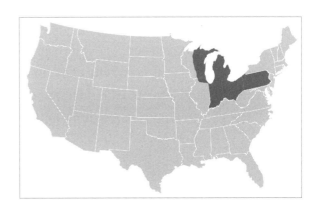

The Industrial North

🎧 19   In comparison with New England and the South, the Industrial North was pluralistic. Successive generations of immigrants flowed into the North from every country in Europe, and later from other continents. Their children went to the same public schools and parents worked in the same offices and factories.

Among those who settled in Pennsylvania, for example, were large groups of Germans. German-speakers became close to one third of the population of Pennsylvania. They became known, confusingly, as "Pennsylvania Dutch", a corruption of the word "Deutsch", meaning "German."

Pennsylvania, Ohio, and Indiana are home to the Amish people, who attract attention when they drive their slow-moving horse-drawn buggies on public roads. They are forced in some states to place "slow-moving vehicle" reflective triangles on their horse-drawn carriages, even if it violates their religious beliefs, because public safety is of paramount concern. However, the Amish are not forced to send their children to public schools, despite a state law that requires all children to attend school through the age of 16. Amish parents can take their children out of school after eighth grade. Most Amish children end their education at that point and begin taking on the responsibilities of a working member of the Amish community.

● NOTES ●

2 **pluralistic**「社会的多元主義の」／ 7 **Pennsylvania Dutch**「ペンシルヴェニア・ダッチ」18 世紀に渡米、移住したドイツ人の子孫。／ 8 **corruption**「訛り」／ 8 **Deutsch**（ドイツ語）「ドイツの」。／ 9 **Amish people** 17 世紀スイスの伝統主義キリスト教会を源とする宗教グループ。主に 18 世紀にアメリカに移住。極めて質素な生活をし、現代文明の多くの便利さを拒否する。／ 11 **place**「置く、設置する」／ 11 **"slow-moving vehicle" reflective triangles**「『低速車両』反射三角板」中がオレンジで周りが赤で縁どられている。／ 15 **through the age of 16**「16 歳まで」＝until.／ 16 **eighth grade**「第 8 学年」日本の中学 2 年。義務教育の年数は州によって違い、大半の州では、6 ～ 16 歳を義務教育としているが、ワシントン D.C. やオレゴンでは 18 歳までと一部例外もある。学年数は、first grade（小学校 1 年）～ twelfth grade（高校 3 年）まで、通しで表されるのが一般的。／ 16 **taking on the responsibilities of …**「…の責任を引き受ける」

Comprehension Check ▶▶▶▶▶▶

1. Which statement is true?
    a. Most of the immigrants who came to America settled in the Industrial North.
    b. New England attracted a large number of German-speaking people.
    c. Horse-drawn buggies are not permitted on public roads.

2. The Amish people in northern states like Pennsylvania ....
   a. choose horse-drawn carriages because it is environmentally friendly.
   b. do not have to send their children to public schools at all.
   c. withdraw from school after they turn 16 years old.*

    The North is sometimes called the "Frost Belt", "Snow Belt" and "Rust Belt." Cold, snowy winters shut down highways, airports, schools, and businesses. The once highly productive industrial heart of America included manufacturing meccas like Detroit, Cleveland, and Pittsburgh. Factory workers with just a high-school education could buy a home, take a summer vacation, and send their children to college. Supported by strong labor unions, the standard of living of manufacturing workers doubled between the end of the war and 1978, with the average forty-year-old worker earning—in today's dollars—$16 an hour. Jobs paid a decent wage for a hard day's work.

    But 1978 was a turning point. Manufacturing employment peaked, the automobile industry began to slump, labor unions lost membership and negotiating power, and companies began to shed workers. Machinery in the factories began to rust from lack of use.

    The Industrial North has suffered more than any other region. It is the one region in the country that is, as a whole, on the decline. When the jobs disappeared, people moved elsewhere. Between the 2000 and 2010 censuses, manufacturing cities lost population. For example, Detroit declined by 25% and Cleveland by 17%.

● NOTES ●
18 **Rust Belt**「錆地帯」斜陽鉄鋼地帯のこと。／21 **Detroit, Cleveland, and Pittsburgh** [pitsbə:rg]「デトロイト」ミシガン州南東部の工業都市。とくに自動車工業で有名。「クリーヴランド」オハイオ州の工業都市、港町。「ピッツバーグ」ペンシルヴェニア州南西部の工業都市。／25 **Jobs paid a decent wage for a hard day's work**「仕事は一日の重労働にみあうかなりの賃金を払った」

Comprehension Check ▶▶▶▶▶

3. One typical characteristic of the Snow Belt is that ....
   a. highways are always kept clear by snow plows.
   b. heavy snows often stop traffic from using highways.
   c. it is different from the area known as the Frost Belt.

🎧 21　　Some northern cities are making a comeback. Large warehouses for "fulfillment centers" of online marketplaces like Amazon and Walmart are opening up in places where large factories used to stand. These online businesses are competing to ship purchases as quickly as possible. Americans order a lot of things online, including bulky items like canoes, refrigerators, and furniture, and the e-commerce companies need lots of space close to where their customers live. To do this, companies are hiring hundreds of thousands of people without college degrees.

　　The new jobs are not in technology hubs; they are in areas with lots of cheap land—and lots of people looking for work. To keep people on the payroll, the companies offer health insurance, retirement plans, and paid time off. Companies hire tens of thousands of seasonal employees for end-of-the-year distribution, but they still need a core of full-time workers throughout the year. The work is hard, but it offers appealing hourly wages. For example, in eastern Pennsylvania, near Bethlehem, a waiter in an ordinary restaurant averages $10.85 an hour. Retail jobs pay an average of $12.67. But a warehouse worker earns an average of $14.46, with an occasional raise and with extra pay for overtime hours.

●NOTES●
35 **fulfillment centers**「配送センター」／36 **Walmart**「ウォルマート」世界中に店舗をもつ世界最大のスーパーマーケットチェーン。／36 **are opening up**「開業している」／36 **in places**「ところどころに」／42 **technology hubs**「テクノロジーの拠点」／43 **on the payroll**「雇われて」payroll「従業員名簿、賃金台帳」／44 **paid time off**「有給休暇」／45 **end-of-the-year distribution**「年末の配送」／48 **Bethlehem** [béθlihəm]「ベスレヘム」／48 **retail jobs**「小売の仕事」

Comprehension Check ▶▶▶▶▶

4. In some northern urban centers, businesses with large warehouses are ....

   a. hiring large numbers of employees.

   b. depending on local factories for goods.

   c. reducing the amount of space they have.

5. Which of the following is NOT a characteristic of these new "fulfillment centers"?

   a. They are located where large plots of land are inexpensive.

   b. The vast majority of the employees are highly educated.

   c. The wages they offer are about the same as retail jobs.

Structure Practice

A. Choose the one underlined word or phrase that should be corrected or rewritten. Then change it so the sentence is correct.

1. There are so many ₁ states that I get ₂ confusing when I ₃ attempt to understand where ₄ events in American history take place.   [   ]

2. Immigrants were able ₁ to reach industrial centers ₂ such as Chicago and Cleveland ₃ in spite the long distances they ₄ had to travel from the Atlantic Coast.
   [   ]

B. Choose the one word or phrase that best completes the sentence.

3. Amish children learn to assume responsibilities step by step and eventually they take .... a farm completely.

    a. away   b. down   c. over   d. out

4. There is little motivation to go to college when factory jobs pay satisfactory ....

    a. earning   b. earnings   c. wage   d. wages

5. If I can take enough .... I'll go to the Rembrandt exhibit in the city museum.

    a. time off   b. time out   c. time over   d. time up

Listening Challenge ▶▶▶▶▶

Listen and fill in the missing words.

1. In [   ] of the Industrial North [   ] a large number of residents with Swedish and Norwegian names and bakeries [   ] Scandinavian breads and pastries.

2. [   ] discriminated against by some Americans, Irish immigrants often depended [   ] get jobs with the police and the fire departments.

3. Due to the cold weather and heavy snow [   ], schools are often closed because school buses [   ] to pick up students.

4. When they retire [   ], many workers in the Rust Belt move to the Sunbelt to avoid shoveling [   ] heating bills in the winter months.

5. With the arrival of new factories and other businesses in this region, there is a large [   ] for the limited number of jobs that will [   ].

◆ Going Further (for discussion or research)

1. What are the benefits of pluralistic society, and what are the disadvantages?

2. Is a college degree essential for every type of job now?

3. Will that change in the future?

CHAPTER 8

ハートランド：大草原と平野

The Heartland: Prairies and Plains

The Heartland: Prairies and Plains

Whether we call it "the Heartland," "Middle America", or "the Midwest" this region includes the prairie states and the plains states. This broad region, divided into two belts, stretches from the Mississippi River west to the foothills of the Rocky Mountains.

The north-south belt along the west side of the Mississippi River comprises the fertile tallgrass prairie states, the heart of what is known as "the Breadbasket." These states grow corn, wheat, and soybeans. Some of the corn becomes feed for cattle and pigs; some goes into the production of ethanol for automotive engines; a lot of it is exported to countries around the world. This is where the trade war with China hurts the farmers.

The north-south belt has extremely good quality soil and plenty of water from multiple rivers. Because their farms are located close to the Mississippi River, farmers in these states can make use of inexpensive barge transportation to get their products to markets downstream and even out into the Atlantic. Few regions in the world have a river system that reaches this far inland. Some 78% of global feed and soybean exports are from the Mississippi Basin, and 60% of all U.S. grain exports travel via the Mississippi River through New Orleans.

● NOTES ●
2 **the prairie states and the plains states**「大草原州と平野州」／ 6 **"the Breadbasket"**「『パンかご』」／ 8 **goes into**　go into ...「…(の状態)になる」／ 13 **make use of ...**「…を利用する」／ 16 **Mississippi Basin**「ミシシッピ川流域」

Comprehension Check ▶▶▶▶▶

1. Which of the following is NOT true?
    a. The prairie states produce barges for transportation.
    b. Ethanol is a product made from corn.
    c. A large portion of soybeans for export are from the area along the Mississippi.

2. Markets for the agricultural products of the prairie states ....
    a. are primarily on the Atlantic Ocean.
    b. can be found around the globe.
    c. are limited to China.

West of the prairie states and stretching west to the foothills of the Rocky Mountains is another north-south belt of the plains states, where elevations are higher, water is less abundant, and the naturally occurring grass is medium to short grass. Once the homeland of the bison that nurtured the Plains Indians, this region is now given over to wheat, cattle, and sheep.

The dividing line between the plains and the prairie states is roughly the 100th meridian, the vertical division halfway across the states of Nebraska and Kansas. That invisible line is about 1,500 feet above sea level. Along that line, the land gets about 25 inches of rainfall per year. To the east there is more rainfall; to the west there is less. At the 100th meridian, there is an even split in men's fashion. West of this line, the percentage of men wearing cowboy hats—symbolic of cattle ranchers—increases. East of this line, the percentage of men wearing freebie baseball caps distributed by agricultural equipment manufacturers and fertilizer companies—symbolic of farmers—dominate.

● NOTES ●
20 **medium to short grass**「中茎から短茎までの草」／21 **is now given over to** give over to …「…に譲る、ひき渡す」／27 **the 100th meridian**「100子午線」西経100度。／29 **freebie baseball caps**「無料でもらえる野球帽」

Comprehension Check ▶▶▶▶▶

3. Which statement is true?
   a. East of the 100th meridian one finds corn.
   b. West of the 100th meridian one finds more water.
   c. East of the 100th meridian one finds more cowboy hats.

4. The plains states are ....
   a. east of the prairie states.
   b. south of the Mississippi River.
   c. between the Rockies and the prairie states.

🎧 24　In this primarily agricultural region, people in small farming communities are the least diverse in the country but neighbors are more likely to keep track of one another's lives and offer help when it is needed. In the 1960s, when the urban centers of America were seen as crime-filled and impersonal, the Heartland came to be perceived as a better place to live. The people of the Heartland, however, continued to feel somehow inferior to the perceived sophistication of California or New York and feel they are ignored by liberal elites.

　　They are skeptical of top-down government, especially the federal government. Frugal by nature and averse to taking on financial risk, however, they feel they have been taken advantage of when the federal government asks them to help bail out Wall Street bankers, insurance companies, and big corporations.

　　They feel the federal taxes they pay are going to minorities, poverty programs, and bilingual education programs for the urban poor. As a result, many of the local people feel that they have a better understanding of how things should be done in their communities than invisible bureaucrats in a dozen different federal agencies in Washington, D.C.

●NOTES●
33 **the least diverse in the country**「国のなかで最も多様性が少ない」／33 **keep track of ...**「…(の動静を) つかんでいる」／37 **the perceived sophistication of California or New York**「(ハートランドの人々が) 認識しているカリフォルニアやニューヨークの洗練性」／39 **skeptical of ...**「…に懐疑的な」／40 **by nature**「生来、生まれつき」／40 **taking on ...**「…を背負い込む」／41 **bail out ...**「…を (資金などを投入して) 救済する」／46 **invisible bureaucrats**「おもてに表れない官僚たち」役所にこもって仕事をしている役人のこと。／46 **a dozen**=a lot of.

Comprehension Check ▶▶▶▶▶

5. The people of communities in the Heartland states ....
    a. take little responsibility for their neighbors.
    b. have little trust in the federal government.
    c. think they are superior to people on the coasts.

Structure Practice

A. Choose the one underlined word or phrase that should be corrected or rewritten. Then change it so the sentence is correct.

1. ₁Access to markets is easier if a farm is ₂locate close to a major river which ₃provides transportation on large ₄barges. [   ]

2. I'm not a person one would ₁refer as being ₂frugal, but I do find it ₃hard to spend money at restaurants that are ₄overly expensive. [   ]

B. Choose the one word or phrase that best completes the sentence.

3. Corn .... a significant portion of the feed given to cattle.
    a. composes   b. comprises   c. consists   d. compounds

4. The prairie states and the plains states are a region where a lot of tornados ....
    a. dominate   b. elevate   c. nurture   d. occur

5. People generally perceive residents in the cities as being .... to help strangers.
    a. diverse   b. skeptical   c. sophisticated   d. unlikely

Listening Challenge ▸▸▸▸▸

Listen and fill in the missing words.

1. There was [   ] in the Heartland and in other regions when it [   ] that corn was being turned into fuel for big cars [   ] used to feed hungry people.

2. The Mississippi River is not just [   ] but it also serves as a place for canoeists, birdwatchers, and fishers to relax [   ].

3. On the [   ] personal experience, I can say that traveling through the prairie states [   ] is rather monotonous, because almost all of the fields [   ].

4. Farm life is lonely, but neighbors [   ] whenever a farm family needs help with a health issue, planting, harvesting [   ].

5. Farmers [   ] to produce a crop, but when [   ], rivers flood, or prices drop, [   ] in debt despite all of their work.

◆ Going Further (for discussion or research)

1. How do Japanese use soybeans?

2. In what ways should governments help farmers and cattle ranchers?

3. What Japanese regions sound similar to the Heartland?

CHAPTER *9* ──────────────── アウトウェスト

Out West

Out West

The elevation and aridity of the Out West between the Rocky Mountains and the Pacific Coast mountains has greatly affected how that region developed. Because it is at an altitude of around 2,000 feet or more and very dry—requiring the drilling of deep wells to provide water for cattle, crops or people—geographic factors resisted the type of agriculture that was possible in the Heartland, where there was sufficient rain for crops and cattle.

Scarcity of water inspired a regional campaign to change nature through a vast network of dams, reservoirs, and canals. Discoveries of oil, coal, and copper drew the interest of investors—invariably from outside the region—and government bureaus wanting to maintain some degree of management over these resources.

First was the 1848–1849 California Gold Rush, giving speculators the nickname "Forty-niners". The gold fields yielded $555 million in a single decade (1848–1858). In 1858, another lode was found in Colorado. Then came discoveries of coal, which even today the mines yield in huge quantities for the production of electricity. It is not unusual for automobile traffic to be backed up waiting at a railroad crossing for long periods of time as trains with five engines pull a hundred cars loaded with coal to market.

● NOTES ●

1 **aridity**「乾燥（状態）」形容詞は arid.／7 **vast network of dams, reservoirs, and canals**「ダム、貯水池、水路の広大に張り巡らされた施設網」／10 **some degree of management**「ある程度までの管理」／12 **the gold fields yielded $555 million**「採金地は5億5500万ドルを産みだした」／14 **in huge quantities**「莫大な量を」／15 **be backed up**「列を作らされる」

Comprehension Check ▸▸▸▸▸▸

1. Which statement is true?

    a. High elevation makes drilling wells easier to accomplish.

    b. What water is available comes through major human efforts.

    c. Water is attained through money paid by individual investors.

2. The discovery of gold ....

    a. occurred in two different states.

    b. came after the discovery of coal.

    c. occurred in the early twentieth century.

For most of the twentieth century, the contiguous states of the "Out West" was probably America's "most strongly imagined" region, replacing New England and the South. For most Americans—who had never actually been there—it was a land of beautiful vistas, Indians, deserts, mountains, national parks, and . . . not much else.

In the 1950s it became the romanticized setting for Western movies and TV series. The cowboy became a hero for at least two generations of kids who had never even seen a horse but were fascinated with the image of the "white hat" hero who always defeated the "black hat" bad guys. In reality, however, together with the flat prairies and plains of the Heartland, it was fly-over country, a big space to fly over between New York and Los Angeles. And it was remote; getting there by land took days by car, bus, or train.

● NOTES ●
18 **contiguous states**「隣接した州たち」the 48 states「（アラスカ、ハワイ以外の）地続きの48州、アメリカ本土」／21 **and … not much else**「そして、…ほかにはあまりない」著者は他にも例をあげようと思ったが思い浮かばず口ごもっている。／22 **setting**「（映画や劇の）背景、道具立て、セット」／26 **fly-over country**「上空通過地域」

Comprehension Check ▶▶▶▶▶

3. Which of the following is NOT true?
    a. In the late twentieth century, most Americans learned a lot about the Out West.
    b. The reality of the Out West region was well known in the twentieth century.
    c. Most Americans traveled over the region by airplane without stopping to see it.

With few exceptions, the Out West is sparsely populated and that has made it a leading candidate for both nuclear testing and nuclear waste dumping. The testing of the first atomic bomb produced by the Manhattan Project was carried out in Alamogordo, New Mexico, on July 16, 1945, prior to the bombing of Hiroshima. The secret government project chose the site because it was remote and there were few people to move out of the testing grounds range. Little attention was given to the radioactivity that remained from that test and others that would follow.

The current nuclear issue is where to permanently dump nuclear waste from around the country. In 1987, the U.S. Congress announced that Yucca Mountain, in Nevada, was the only location that would be studied for a national repository for high-level nuclear waste and spent nuclear fuel. All of the final candidate locations were in the Out West, but they chose Yucca to be the site.

The plan faced stiff opposition from Nevada residents, environmentalists, and local government officials. The project was defunded by President Obama in 2012, but in 2017, the controversial, long-dormant plan to permanently store nuclear waste underground at Yucca Mountain was back in the news. President Trump reopened that discussion.

●NOTES●

29 **is sparsely populated**「（人・動物が）まばらに住む」／31 **the Manhattan Project**「マンハッタン計画」第二次大戦中のアメリカ陸軍の原子爆弾開発計画。／32 **Alamogordo**「アラモゴード」ニュー・メキシコ州南部の市。世界最初の原爆実験が付近の砂漠でおこなわれた。／34 **move out of the testing grounds range**「実験場の範囲外に移住する」／35 **others that would follow**「続くことになる他の実験たち」／39 **location**「選定地、立地」／42 **was defunded**　defund「資金を引き揚げる」／43 **controversial**「物議をかもす、論争の的となる」／43 **long-dormant plan**「長期休眠計画」dormant「活動しない、潜伏している」／44 **was back in the news**「ニュースで再び騒がれる、紙上でまた騒がれる」

Comprehension Check ▷▷▷▷▷▷

4. What was the reason for placing the nuclear testing grounds in the Out West?
    a. Nuclear radioactivity was a major concern, so the government tested underground.
    b. New Mexico was close to the Pacific, making transportation easier.
    c. It was far away from large populations and residents could easily be moved out.

5. What plan is controversial particularly in the state of Nevada?
    a. The plan to build storage for nuclear waste.
    b. The plan to build a memorial to the Manhattan Project.
    c. A plan that would damage the beautiful Yucca Mountain area.

Structure Practice ▶▶▶▶▶

A. Choose the one underlined word or phrase that should be corrected or rewritten. Then change it so the sentence is correct.

1. Due to ₁arid conditioning in the higher ₂mountain ranges, it is ₃next to impossible to ₄raise crops like those of the Heartland. [   ]

2. Boys who ₁grew up in the 1950s were ₂fascinating by the cowboys they saw on TV programs who ₃fought against evil characters and ₄stood up for good people. [   ]

B. Choose the one word or phrase that best completes the sentence.

3. Enormous coal, copper, and bauxite mines have .... attention from companies hoping to profit from these natural resources.

    a. attracted   b. drawn   c. resisted   d. yielded

4. Support for protection of the environment is .... in areas where natural resources provide well-paying jobs like mining.

    a. remote   b. replaced   c. scarce   d. spent

5. Examination of potential sites for building dams and reservoirs is .... the government.

    a. carried out   b. chosen to   c. required by   d. studied for

Out West   53

Listening Challenge ▶▶▶▶▶

Listen and fill in the missing words.

1. Recently it seems that there is [   ] news in the newspapers about huge fires in the forests [   ] of the western states.

2. As a child, my father and I [   ] journeys by car from our home in the South to see the national parks [   ].

3. Some states [   ] solar power and wind power, but [   ] store electricity and to transmit it [   ].

4. [   ] in the Out West is scattered, it is [   ] schools, medical treatment, and [   ] to everyone.

5. The term NIMBY, "not in my backyard," [   ] people do not want dangerous or polluting activities in the area [   ] they live.

◆ Going Further (for discussion or research)

1. Have you seen places in this region in movies? Can you remember the titles of the movies?

2. Where do you think each country should put nuclear waste and spent nuclear fuel?

CHAPTER 10

アラスカ

Alaska

Alasaka

Alaska is unique. First, the land area is enormous and there is lots of water. Second, the state is one-fifth the size of all of the Lower 48 states combined: 570,640 square miles. In contrast, the population is a mere 741,894 as of 2016. Some 15.2% identify themselves as either American Indian or Alaska Native.

The mountain ranges and strong rivers make access by road entirely impossible. Helicopters are suitable for short-distance access, but in the bush, there are few flat, open spaces for the helicopter to land. Because there is no way to bring in fuel, the helicopters have to bring their own fuel as well.

Small planes allow middle-range access, but there are few landing strips for them to touch down. Seaplanes—with pontoons that allow them to land on the surface of a lake when there is no strong wind—are suitable for a few passengers but not for huge quantities of supplies. Hampering all air transportation are changeable weather conditions. Fog, heavy rain, lightning, wind, and flooding can prevent any aircraft from reaching its destination, or returning from that destination.

● NOTES ●
2 **the Lower 48 states** アラスカ州を除くアメリカ合衆国の大陸48州。／3 **square miles** square mile「平方マイル」square meter「平方メートル」／3 **as of 2016**「2016年現在」／5 **by road**「陸路で、自動車で」／8 **bring in**「持ち込む」／8 **as well**「そのうえ、おまけに」／10 **touch down**「着陸する」／10 **pontoon** 水上機のフロート。

Comprehension Check ▷▷▷▷▷

1. Which statement is NOT true?
    a. Alaska is five times larger than any other state.
    b. Some fifteen percent of the residents are Alaska Native or American Indian.
    c. The least suitable way to travel is by road.

2. Air transportation within Alaska is ....
    a. easiest by small plane.
    b. highly dependent on places to take off and land.
    c. safest by water and road.

Alaska's economy began with large outside enterprises such as salmon-packing firms began exploiting the salmon fisheries. But because the necessary capital came from other states, these firms paid few taxes. And they brought in not only their own fishermen but also their own cannery crews. Following these initial operations, the Alaska Gold Rush at Nome in 1896 brought an entirely different group into the mix of the population.

By 1941, Alaska had a population of only 72,000, but during World War II, population growth accelerated. The war revolutionized Alaska because it was in a strategic location. Thousands of troops were rushed north while army and navy bases were built in places like Kodiak Island, Sitka, Anchorage, and Fairbanks.

In the summer of 1942 Japanese forces invaded the Aleutian chain and American armed forces began intensive efforts to oust them, finally succeeding in the autumn of 1943. Federal activities declined sharply after the war ended in 1945, but resumed again with the outbreak of the Cold War. By 1950 the number of military personnel had increased to 138,000. Then came the discovery of North America's largest oil field on Alaska public land.

● NOTES ●

15 **salmon-packing firms**「鮭の缶詰会社」／16 **But because the necessary capital came from other states, these firms paid few taxes.**「資金も他の州からきているため、これらの企業は地元には税金をあまり払わなかった」アラスカに進出した企業の資金は他の州の銀行などの出資によるものだった。／18 **the Alaska Gold Rush at Nome in 1896** アラスカ州西端のノームで1896年に金鉱が発見されゴールドラッシュになった。／24 **Kodiak Island, Sitka, Anchorage, and Fairbanks**「コディアック島」はアラスカ湾の島。「シトゥカ」はアラスカ湾南東部アレグサンダー諸島にある町。「アンカレッジ」は南部にあるアラスカ最大の市で海港、空港を備える。「フェアバンクス」アラスカ中央部東寄りにある市、鉄道と高速道路の終点になっている。／25 **the Aleutian chain**「アリューシャン列島」その形状が鎖の様につながっていることから。／26 **oust**「追い出す、駆逐する」／27 **Federal activities**「連邦政府の活動」／27 **resumed**「取り戻す」／28 **the Cold War**「冷戦」第2次世界大戦後のアメリカとソ連を中心に繰り広げられた敵対関係。ベルリンの壁の崩壊後1カ月の1989年12月の米ソの会談で冷戦終結が宣言された。

Comprehension Check ▶▶▶▶▶

3. Salmon-packing firms in Alaska ....
   a. significantly benefited the local population.
   b. used imported technology in order to make profits.
   c. depended on outside investment and workers from outside.

🎧 30 Given the resources that have been discovered in Alaska—gold, silver, molybdenum, and petroleum—the battle over the right to exploit those potentially valuable resources became heated. To get at the petroleum, for example, every resident would have to be cleared off the land—including the Native Peoples. This was and continues to be seriously affected by the Alaska Native Claims Settlement Act (ANCSA). And even if the extraction facilities are permitted, where would the profit go?

Today both Native and white residents of the state feel that the federal government is taking far too much land out of their hands. They feel that whenever decisions are made about land and resources, people from Texas, California and New York—states with larger numbers of members in the U.S. House of Representatives—carry more weight than people from Alaska—which has only one representative.

One camp wants to exploit the seemingly endless resources for the benefit of the residents of the state. Why, they ask, should the federal government prohibit the residents from gaining benefits from, for example, the pumping of petroleum at Prudhoe Bay?

Another camp wants to keep the largest remaining wilderness in the U.S. intact for future generations. Their aim is to basically block any and all exploitation of the land.

● NOTES ●

31 **molybdenum** [məlíbdənəm]「モリブデン」融点が高く、熱膨張率が低く、熱伝導性が高い利点がある、さまざまな工業用途に欠かすことのできない金属材料。／33 **get at ...**「…を手に入れる」／34 **This was and continues to be seriously affected by ...**「…によって真剣に影響されたし（これからも）され続ける」／35 **Alaska Native Claims Settlement Act (ANCSA)**「アラスカ先住民請求和解法 (ANCSA)」1971年12月にニクソン大統領によって調印され、米国史上最大の土地請求和解となった。ANCSA は、アラスカの先住民の土地所有権をめぐる長年の問題の解決とアラスカ全体の経済発展を促進することを目的とした。／36 **extraction facilities**「（石油などを）採取する施設、設備」／40 **the U.S. House of Representatives**「アメリカ下院」日本の衆議院。上院は the Senate。／40 **carry more weight**「より大きい影響力がある」／42 **camp**「（政治的な主義主張などを同じにする）グループ、同士」／45 **Prudhoe Bay**「プルドーベイ」アラスカ州北部北極海の沿岸に位置するアメリカ最大級の油田 (oil field) の中心地。／46 **keep ... inact**「…をそのままにしておく」intact「無傷で」

Comprehension Check ▷▷▷▷▷

4. What have been among the effects of exploiting Alaska's resources?
    a. Residents have to move off of their lands.
    b. All profits go to the state government.
    c. Local petroleum prices have gone down.

5. Which of the following is NOT promoted by a group of local people?
    a. Giving more land to the federal government.

b. Sharing profits from resources with local residents.

c. Protecting wilderness for people of the future.

Structure Practice

A. Choose the one underlined word or phrase that should be corrected or rewritten. Then change it so the sentence is correct.

1. Although a federal law may ₁allowing companies to ₂exploit resources, a state law may be ₃established to ₄prevent them from doing so.   [   ]

2. ₁Constructing air strips in the north in order to ₂gain access to petroleum has been seen as ₃cause a severe damage to both the land and the animal population that ₄travels through the area.   [   ]

B. Choose the one word or phrase that best completes the sentence.

3. Seaplane pilots have to contend with ....

    a. large numbers of passengers.
    b. heavy winds during landing and take-off.
    c. large quantities of equipment and supplies.
    d. long-range flight times.

4. During World War II, Alaska ....

    a. revolutionized the army.
    b. lost a significant part of its population.
    c. had its largest population.
    d. was in a strategic location.

5. In regard to its valuable resources, both Native Alaskans and white Alaskans ....

    a. feel too many decisions are out of their control.
    b. worry about where they will move if resources disappear.
    c. prohibit discussion of the issue in local government.
    d. have no concern about the future of the state.

Listening Challenge ▶▶▶▶▶

Listen and fill in the missing words.

1. Fishing for trout and salmon is not [   ] the Native Alaskans [   ] but also a way for sportsmen to [   ].

2. After [   ] in a seaplane, the group [   ] a beautiful lake [   ] where there were several cabins and lodges [   ].

3. Pumping petroleum [   ] at Prudhoe Bay is one potential [   ], but a [   ] the long pipeline that carries the petroleum [   ] wilderness areas.

4. Bush pilots who fly seaplanes [   ] periods without a day off and [   ] with no work to do.

5. Some Alaskans [   ] the last place in the U.S. [   ] can test himself or herself against the environment and be [   ] the rest of the world.

◆ Going Further (for discussion or research)

1. What is your image of the huge state of Alaska?

2. What do you know about the Native People of Alaska?

3. Why will Alaska be important in the future?

CHAPTER 11 ──────────── 太平洋岸北西部

The Pacific Northwest

The Pacific Northwest

The Pacific Northwest, along the West Coast from just south of San Francisco north to Seattle, was settled by merchants, missionaries, and woodsmen from New England. They came by boat, in the days before wagons first conquered the high mountains of the West. Portland, Oregon, was founded in 1845 by New England traders who had come all the way around South America's Cape Horn. Their aim was to trade with Alaska and countries on the Pacific Ocean. Seattle, as a maritime, export-based city, also looked toward Asia and Alaska rather than to the rest of America.

Bringing with them New England intellectualism, idealism, and utopianism, they laid down the foundation for a culture of individual fulfillment. Currently in the Pacific Northwest this continues as a strong cultural liberalism. The people of the region maintain a willingness to let others follow their own paths and to support a progressive philosophy.

The second stage of immigration started with fur traders and farmers who traveled the hard way—across the land by horse and wagon—from Appalachia and elsewhere. They brought a completely different set of ideas and customs and settled inland. Today there is friction between city dwellers and these rural residents who complain that the city residents are telling them where they can build, what trees they can cut, and how many guns they can own.

● NOTES ●

4 **Portland**「ポートランド」オレゴン州北西部の港市。／5 **Cape Horn**「ホーン岬」南米最南端にある岬。強風と荒波で航行の難所。ちなみに大西洋と太平洋を結ぶパナマ運河の開通は1914年。／6 **Seattle**「シアトル」ワシントン州北西部にある同州最大の都市。／9 **laid down** lay down「築く、建造する、敷設する」／10 **individual fulfillment**「個人の確立」／21 **thoroughness**「徹底」thorough「完全な、徹底的な」

Comprehension Check ▶▶▶▶▶

1. Which do you think is true from the information above?
    a. Appalachian immigrants brought utopian ideas to the Pacific Northwest.
    b. The earliest immigrants did not arrive by horse and wagon.
    c. Residents of the cities and rural areas today share common ways of thinking.

2. The immigrants from New England focused on ....
    a. trade with areas on the Pacific.
    b. trade with other parts of the U.S.
    c. trade routes crossing the mountains.

Protection of the environment and a thoroughness in recycling are combined in states' laws that ban pop-top cans and throwaway bottles. Oregon was the first state in the country—later followed by the other states in the region—to require a deposit on returnable bottles, raising the purchase price but encouraging recycling.

All three states of the Pacific Northwest struggle over logging rights. The lumber industry is particularly powerful in Oregon, but throughout the region there is serious discord between loggers who want freer access to timber and anti-logging "tree-huggers," who believe that forests should be kept as they are for future generations and to protect other species of plants and animals.

A recent case in California involved the proposed expansion of the Redwood National Park, near Eureka, California, which brought opposition from loggers who would lose high-paying jobs as a result. To the loggers, understandably, reserving land for tourists and backpackers from outside the area was hardly as important as freedom to log and earn a paycheck to keep food on the table. The clash over environmental issues is illustrated elsewhere by the Federal Way school district in exurban Seattle. In 2007, the school board there banned the showing of Al Gore's global warming documentary, *An Inconvenient Truth*.

● NOTES ●

19 **are combined in ...**「…に組み合わされている」／20 **pop-top cans and throwaway bottles**「引きあげ式のふたがついた缶と使い捨てのボトル」／21 **a deposit on returnable bottles**「回収可能なボトルに課す保証金」／23 **All three states of the Pacific Northwest** 北から、ワシントン州、オレゴン州、カリフォルニア州。／25 **tree-huggers**「樹木保全派」hug「大事に守る；ハグする」／28 **Redwood National Park**「レッドウッド国立公園」正式名称は Redwood National and State Parks. カリフォルニア州最北端に位置し、太平洋沿い南北約 55km、東京ドームのおよそ 9,100 倍の広大な面積 (425k㎡) を有する公園。1980 年に特徴的な生態系が評価され、また世界的にも貴重な森を保護するため、世界遺産に登録された。／29 **Eureka** [juəríːkə]「ユーリカ」サンフランシスコとポートランドの中間地点にある都市。／29 **brought opposition**「反対をもたらした」／30 **To the loggers**「伐木作業者にとっては」／34 **exurban**「準郊外の」exurb は郊外 (suburb) よりさらに都市を離れて広がる高級住宅街。／34 **school board**「教育委員会」／34 **Al Gore**「アル・ゴア」アメリカ元副大統領でノーベル平和賞受賞者。環境問題を訴えるドキュメンタリー映画 *An Inconvenient Truth*『不都合な真実』(2007) でアカデミー賞「長編ドキュメンタリー賞」を受賞。

Comprehension Check ▶▶▶▶▶

3. Which environmental issue is especially controversial in the region?
   a. A ban on throwaway bottles and cans.
   b. Movies describing backcountry hiking paths.
   c. The right to cut timber in the forests.

🎧 33　Although a lot of attention is given to Silicon Valley, Seattle is another area that has drawn young people, especially the millennial-age group, ages 25 to 34. Its percentage of millennials is nearly the highest in America among big cities, according to the national census estimates for 2015.

　　In that year, it was one of the highest-ranking cities in America in terms of drawing young workers. One reason is that Seattle passed the nation's first big-city $15-per-hour minimum wage law. It is the home for headquarters of the outdoors specialist Eddie Bauer, the coffee purveyor Starbucks, the aircraft manufacturer Boeing, the superstore chain Costco, the computer software pioneer Microsoft, and a conglomerate auspiciously named Amazon.

　　Thirty years ago, Seattle was filled with dilapidated warehouses, crumbling docks, a seedy residential and commercial district on the edge of downtown, and an old rail yard. Today it has been rehabilitated to host scores of small startups. New buildings house internet and software companies. The commercial district has become a cool zip code, with well-designed offices and condominiums appearing one after another. Gourmet restaurants and new cultural venues have taken over abandoned buildings and street-level parking lots.

●NOTES●
36 **Silicon Valley**「シリコン・ヴァレー」サンフランシスコの南東にある IT 関連産業が集まった渓谷地帯。／37 **millennial-age group, ages 25 to 34**　millennial-age group とはアメリカで 1980 年代半ばから 2003 年の間に生まれた世代。あるいは、2000 年 (millennium) 以降に成人または社会人になる世代を指す。幼少期からデジタル機器に親しむ。ここでの 25 歳から 34 歳という年齢は 2015 年時点の年齢。／41 **passed**　pass「（法案を）承認する、可決する」／43 **Eddie Bauer**「エディーバウアー」アメリカのファッションブランド、およびその創設者。／43 **purveyor**　purvey「（食料などを）提供する、調達する」／44 **Costco**「コストコ」会員制倉庫型スーパーマーケットの名前。／44 **a conglomerate auspiciously named Amazon**「おめでたくアマゾンと名づけられた巨大複合企業」／46 **dilapidated**「荒れはてた、老朽化した」／46 **crumbling**　crumble「ぼろぼろに崩れる」／47 **a seedy residential and commercial district**「怪しげな住まいと怪しげな商売の地域」／47 **rail yard**「鉄道の操車場」／48 **host**「受け入れる」／48 **startup**「新興企業、ベンチャー企業」／49 **house ...**　動詞「…に宿を貸す、場所を提供する」／52 **street-level parking lots**「路面の駐車場」建物になっていない駐車用地。

Comprehension Check ▷▷▷▷▷

4. Millennial Americans are particularly drawn to ....
    a. urban areas with headquarters of large companies.
    b. areas where logging is prohibited.
    c. cities with lower minimum wage laws

5. The attractiveness of Seattle does not include
   a. seedy residential districts.
   b. lots of startup companies.
   c. sophisticated offices and restaurants.

Structure Practice

A. Choose the one underlined word or phrase that should be corrected or rewritten. Then change it so the sentence is correct.

1. Early settlers in the Pacific Northwest were ₁willing to ₂make other people ₃live ₄according to their own ideas. [   ]

2. Laws ₁guaranteeing a high minimum wage ₂draw out a lot of younger workers to major industries ₃such as Microsoft and Amazon and ₄outdoor specialist Eddie Bauer. [   ]

B. Choose the one word or phrase that best completes the sentence.

3. Parents who have learned how to earn money .... are often impatient with their children who don't see the need to work hard.
   a. after trouble   b. by difficulty   c. in struggles   d. the hard way

4. .... anything was left for us to eat.
   a. Basically   b. Hardly   c. Nearly   d. Sadly

5. Couples usually do their best to choose a day that is .... for their wedding ceremony.
   a. advantageous   b. auspicious   c. beneficial   d. encouraging

Listening Challenge

Listen and fill in the missing words.

1. When making a decision [   ] to Oregon or not, I [   ] the opportunities nearby for hiking, fishing, and skiing.

2. What [   ] short-term visit to Seattle turned out to [   ] a long-term career [   ] a love affair with the area around Mount Rainier.

3. The unpleasantness [   ] urban residents and people in the countryside is [   ] different ideas about life styles.

4. Three [   ] downtown Seattle was [   ], with empty buildings [   ], homeless people everywhere, and no businesses for young workers.

5. In the Pacific Northwest, there is [   ] high-tech industries and protected [   ], which gives the impression of [   ] more than enough space for everyone.

◆ Going Further (for discussion or research)

1. What kinds of work did early Japanese immigrants (Issei) do in the Pacific Northwest?

2. Where is Mount St. Helens and what happened there in 1980?

3. Do you purchase products from companies based in the Pacific Northwest?

CHAPTER  　　　　　　　　　　　　　　　　　　　　南西部

The Southwest

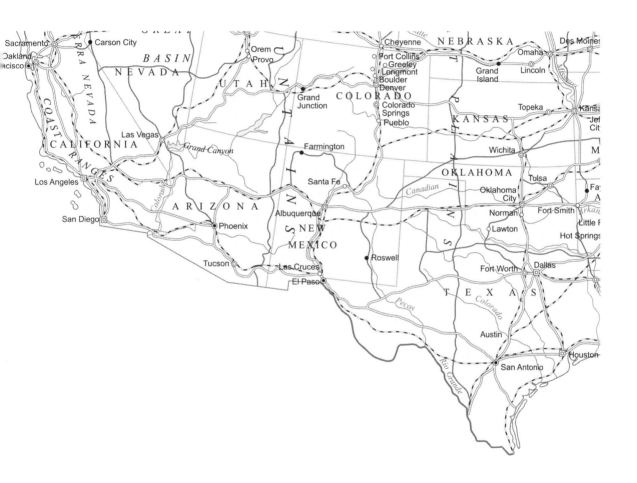

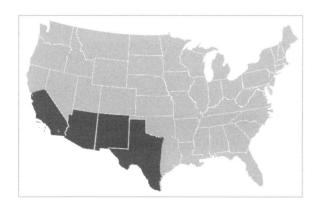

The Southwest

🎧 34   The North American continent was explored and colonized by the British, the French and the Spanish—and the Spanish were the first to meet the Native Americans. The territory that the Spanish occupied include the Southwest, which is southwest Texas, New Mexico, southern Arizona, and southern California. They called it Mexico. 5

Two historical events serve to indicate just how long this region was "Mexican." One is that what is now Santa Fe was the capital city of the Kingdom of New Mexico approximately ten years before the Pilgrims set foot on Plymouth Rock. A second is that between 1769 and 1823, Franciscan missionaries from Mexico established a chain of 21 missions along what is now the California coastline, several of which are 10 major cities today.

The earliest was San Diego, now a major U.S. naval base, followed by important missions that evolved into Los Angeles, Santa Barbara, and one of the most popular tourist destinations in America: San Francisco. All have Spanish names, and all originated as small mission-centered communities, where Spanish-speaking priests 15 gathered members of the local tribes of Native Americans and tried to convert that population to Christianity. The coastal boundary between the Southwest and the Pacific Northwest is the mission town of San Luis Obispo.

● NOTES ●
7 **Santa Fe**「サンタフェ」ニューメキシコ州中北部の市。／7 **the Kingdom of New Mexico**「ニューメキシコ」とはスペイン語の「新しいメキシコ」が英語化されたもの。1540年にスペイン人が探検を始め1598年から入植がはじまり、1610年にサンタフェを首都とした。その後、アメリカとメキシコ戦争の結果、ニューメキシコは1848年にカリフォルニア州と共にメキシコから割譲され、1912年に合衆国の第47番目の州となった。／8 **Pilgrims set foot on Plymouth Rock** ピルグリムファーザーズが1620年にはじめてプリマスに上陸したこと。／9 **Franciscan missionaries**「フランシスコ修道会の宣教師」／9 **a chain of 21 missions**「一連の21教区」／12 **San Diego**「サンディエゴ」カリフォルニア州南部に位置する市。／13 **evolved into ...**「…に徐々に発展した」／13 **Santa Barbara**「サンタバーバラ」ロスアンジェルス北部に位置する市。／18 **San Luis Obispo**「サンルイスオビスポ」サンフランシスコとロスアンジェルスの中間に位置する市。

Comprehension Check ▷▷▷▷▷▷

1. Which statement is true?

    a. The first European colony in the U.S. was in the Southwest.

    b. Franciscan missionaries from Mexico set up missions along the Atlantic.

    c. San Diego is a mission town founded before the Pilgrims arrived.

2. A chain of missions was established ....

   a. just on the Mexican coast.

   b. which tried to convert local Indians.

   c. ending in Los Angeles.

While Spanish-speaking people from many countries live in major cities like New York City and Chicago, the greatest concentration is in the Southwest. According to the most recent U.S. Census Bureau (2010), in the broad Southwest, the Hispanic population is far above the average for the United States. The national average is 16.3% Hispanic, but in these states, the percentages often rise over 50%. According to the U.S. Census Bureau, the U.S. population is 38% nonwhite now. In three states of the Southwest—California, Texas, and New Mexico—the majority is already nonwhite.

In the Southwest, the particular percentage of Asians and Hispanics is important. In 2015, across America, that combination was 18% Hispanic and 6% Asian, and projected percentages for the whole country in 2035 will be 9% Asian and 21% Hispanic. The percentage of white residents will fall to 55%, and continue to fall. That phenomenon will be particularly prominent in the Southwest.

This region is characterized both by long-established Spanish-speaking communities mixed in among Anglo communities and by large increases in the number of Spanish-speaking immigrants. The once-a-decade national census has until now categorized these people as "Hispanic," a term that is not entirely satisfactory but continues to be used to categorize everyone from Puerto Ricans to Colombians to Mexicans.

● NOTES ●
21 **the most recent U.S. Census Bureau (2010)**「最新のアメリカ国勢調査（局）」アメリカの国勢調査は10年ごとに行われるので本書が執筆された2019年の時点では2010年の調査が最新となる。／22 **average for …**「…の平均」／28 **In 2015**　2015年の数字はアメリカ国勢調査とPew Reserch Centerの発表資料による。／32 **is characterized both by**　be characterized by …「…に特徴がある」／33 **mixed in**「交わる」／33 **Anglo**「白人のアメリカ人」／34 **once-a-decade**「10年に一回の」decade「10年間、10個」／36 **Puerto Ricans** [pwèrtə ríːkn]「プエルトリコ人」Puerto Rico「プエルトリコ」

Comprehension Check ▷▷▷▷▷▷

3. Today the percentage of Hispanics ....

   a. is much higher in the Southwest than the average across the nation.

The Southwest 69

b. and other nonwhites is less than half in New Mexico.
　　c. in the Southwest is double that of Asians.

🎧 36　Many Americans see Texas and California as opposites. While California votes Democrat, is environmentally friendly, and believes government should provide lots of services, Texas votes Republican, believes that natural resources are to be exploited, and wants to cut government services to a minimum.

　　This was quite apparent in Houston as a result of the 2017 Hurricane Harvey disaster in Texas. Houston had been built on an upbeat, pro-business strategy of low taxes and small government and had become the fourth largest metropolis in the country. It had become a world energy capital with strong suits in medicine, electronics, space (NASA), engineering, finance, and law. Until Harvey at least, no local politicians or businesspeople wanted to impose restrictions on growth by taxing businesses in order to pay for infrastructure. Many Texans regarded this as the key to real prosperity and an America unregulated by the federal government.

　　But the downside was less money spent on schools, welfare, and police, and less money on much-needed infrastructure like roads, drainage canals, water mains, bridges, and levees. As a result, Houston was completely unprepared for the heavy rains and flooding that hit the city. The main highways passing through the city center turned into rivers and even the expensive neighborhoods took in several meters of water.

●NOTES●
40 **services**「（行政）事業」／42 **Houston** [hjústn]「ヒューストン」テキサス州南東部の市。NASA (National Aeronautics and Space Administration) がある。／42 **2017 Hurricane Harvey disaster**「ハリケーン・ハービー」は、2017年8月末にテキサス州を襲った大型ハリケーン。アメリカ災害史上2番目に大きい損害を与えた。／43 **pro-business**「企業を向いた、企業優先の」pro-「支持の、賛成の、ひいきの」／45 **suit** [súːt]「背広組；専門職の人」／47 **impose restrictions on growth**「成長に制限を加える」／48 **pay for infrastructure**「インフラにお金を使う」infrastructure 水道、電気、ガス、交通機関などの社会の基本的設備。／48 **Texan** [téksn]「テキサス州の人」／49 **an America**「アメリカの一員」／54 **expensive neighborhoods**「高級住宅地」

Comprehension Check ▶▶▶▶▶

4. Which of the following is NOT true?
　　a. People in Texas lean toward the Republicans in elections.
　　b. Pro-business voters are more common in Texas.
　　c. Residents in California tend to vote to reduce taxes and government services.

5. What is one of the negative effects of reducing local taxes?
   a. Local business are more prosperous.
   b. Infrastructure is maintained to a lesser degree.
   c. Schools and welfare programs are financed by the federal government.

Structure Practice

A. Choose the one underlined word or phrase that should be corrected or rewritten. Then change it so the sentence is correct.

1. In terms of the ₁ mixture of the population Metropolitan New York and the Southwest ₂ are similar, but ₃ in most other ways they are complete ₄ opposition.

   [   ]

2. Many ₁ contemporary urban centers in the Southwest ₂ involved from missions and government communities ₃ founded during ₄ the era of the Kingdom of Mexico.

   [   ]

B. Choose the one word or phrase that best completes the sentence.

3. Cities that were once .... by small stores and factories now host headquarters for multinational corporations, upscale restaurants, and medical research centers.

   a. founded   b. occupied   c. originated   d. provided

4. Various think tanks .... that by 2035 nonwhite residents of the U.S. will rise to approximately 45%.

   a. categorize   b. concentrate   c. originate   d. project

5. Californians are not afraid to .... regulations on businesses in order to protect the environment for future generations.

   a. combine   b. exploit   c. impose   d. restrict

The Southwest 71

Listening Challenge ▸▸▸▸▸▸

Listen and fill in the missing words.

1. Southwest Texas [   ] cattle, oil, finance, and high-tech business, [   ] is considered to be part of the Deep South.

2. San Diego's Old Town [   ] tourists, but the city also has an excellent zoo and [   ] naval base where several aircraft carriers [   ].

3. Although [   ] Spanish speakers do not try to learn English, [   ], Spanish speakers do try, because they [   ] asset in looking for work.

4. Houston is vulnerable [   ] it is in a low-lying plain, near the Gulf of Mexico, and in the pathway of [   ].

5. The image [   ] Texans is that they wear a cowboy hat and fancy boots, but [   ] that those who dress that way may be businesspeople [   ] with cows, horses, and a ranch.

◆ Going Further (for discussion or research)

1. What kind of land stretches across the Southwest?

2. Do you think all Americans need to speak English?

CHAPTER *13* ───ハワイ

Hawaii

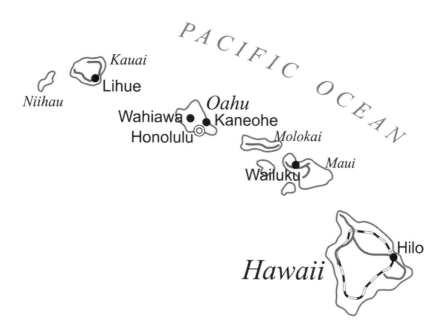

Hawaii

The diversity of Hawaii results from wave after wave of immigrants. First, came the Europeans and the Americans. Then came successive waves of immigrant workers, hired to work on the sugar cane and pineapple plantations. Workers from different countries, speaking different languages, learned to communicate in a pidgin language in order to get work done. Eventually the local pidgin, called Hawaii Creole English, absorbed words from all of these languages, including Hawaiian, English, Japanese, Chinese, and Tagalog. It became a mark of belonging. As an aside, Hawaii is the only state in the country to have two official languages: Hawaiian and English.

Today there is no majority ethnic group. Intermarriage between races and ethnic groups is higher in Hawaii than any other state. Some 42% of newlyweds in Hawaii between 2008 and 2010 were intermarried. Compare this with cities in the Deep South, where that figure is only 3%.

The highest rates of intermarried white and Asian couples are in Hawaii where they are 9% of the population. The "Asian alone" or "Asian in combination" population represented 56.1% of the total population of Hawaii according to the Vintage 2014 Population Estimates from the U.S. Census Bureau.

● NOTES ●
3 **sugar cane**「サトウキビ」／4 **pidgin language**「混合言語」／5 **get work done**「仕事をやり遂げる」／7 **Tagalog**「タガログ語」フィリッピンの公用語。／7 **As an aside**「余談として」／9 **Intermarriage** 異なる人種・階級・氏族・宗教の人の結婚。／10 **newlyweds**「新婚夫婦、新婚さん」通例複数形で使う。／14 **Asian in combination**「組合せの片方がアジア系」／15 **the Vintage 2014 Population Estimates**「2014 年人口推計」vintage は特定の年度を表すのに使う。

Comprehension Check ▶▶▶▶▶

1. Which statement is true?
    a. Hawaiian pidgin is one of the official languages of the state.
    b. Pidgin includes words from at least five different languages.
    c. Hawaii Creole English was not used in the workplaces of the islands.

2. Intermarriage between races and ethnic groups in Hawaii between 2008 and 2010 ....
    a. was far less common between than in other states.
    b. was more than four out of ten couples.
    c. doubled the number in the Deep South.

🎧 38　Native Hawaiians to one degree or another still resent the fact that the Kingdom of Hawaii was overthrown by white immigrants from the American mainland in 1893. The Republic of Hawaii was annexed by the U.S. in 1896 as a territory, and the U.S. government took ownership of more than two million acres of crown and government lands that had belonged to the republic and the kingdom. What came to be known as the Big Five companies collaborated with the U.S. to rule Hawaii with a government composed of outsiders.

　The U.S. government made Hawaii the 50th state in 1959. But the Native Hawaiians are still living in poverty and occupying the lowest rung on the socio-economic ladder of the islands. They have a high incarceration rate, very little land ownership, and poor education.

　In an effort to counter this, a rediscovery of Hawaiian culture began in the 1970s. Called the Hawaiian Renaissance, this movement, stimulated in part by the African American Civil Rights Movement, included a rediscovery of Hawaiian culture. Local people began to take pride in speaking Hawaiian pidgin and there was a boom in the study of Hawaiian language and culture. The Renaissance also included popularity of slack-key guitar music, partly sung in Hawaiian, by the legendary Gabby Pahinui and various other groups. It also included a renewed interest in authentic hula, myths, and chants.

●NOTES●
17 **to one degree or another**「多少は、いささか」／19 **was annexed by**「併合された」annex「併合する、横取りする」／22 **the Big Five companies**「ビッグ・ファイブ（企業群）」20世紀初頭に台頭し1960年代に至るまでハワイ州の政治・経済を牛耳ってきた大手砂糖会社を筆頭とする複合企業群。1970年代に入り砂糖のプランテーションが次々に閉鎖されると、これらビッグ・ファイブの傘下にあった企業は他州の企業に買収・合併されていった。／25 **socio-economic ladder**「社会的経済的階層」／29 **in part**「一部分、部分的に」=partly／29 **the African American Civil Rights Movement**　アフリカ系アメリカ人の自由と権利を求めて主に1950年代から1960年代にかけて行われた運動で「公民権運動」と呼ばれる。1963年5月合衆国連邦最高裁はアラバマ州バーミンガム市の人種隔離条例を違憲とする判決を下した。同年8月にはキング牧師の"I have a dream"の演説で有名なワシントン大行進があった。その後も黒人の尊厳を求める運動は続いた。／33 **slack-key guitar**　ギターの種類ではなく、ハワイで生まれたギターの弾き方の呼び名。ウクレレやスチール・ギターが登場するよりも以前からハワイで一部の人の間で伝えられていた。／33 **Gabby Pahinui**「ギャビー・パヒヌイ」1950年頃からスラッキー・ギターの演奏活動を積極的に行った。／34 **hula** [húːlə]「フラダンス、フラ音楽」／35 **chant**「詠唱歌」

Comprehension Check ▶▶▶▶▶

3. The Republic of Hawaii ....
    a. had never been an actual kingdom.
    b. appeared before the Kingdom of Hawaii.
    c. became a U.S. territory.

4. A movement known as the Hawaiian Renaissance ....

   a. developed pride in the local pidgin and the study of Hawaiian language.

   b. overlooked music performed in the Hawaiian language.

   c. paid little attention to myths of the Hawaiian tradition.

    Residents in Honolulu fall into two categories. One is the group that has settled in Hawaii after they have made money elsewhere or that has significant sources of income from investments that do not require a well-paying job in Hawaii. These residents can afford to buy and maintain new condominiums or large houses in the better parts of the city. They do not have to worry about too many things.

    The other group is the working class, who struggle to pay rent for even minimal housing with each adult member of the family working at jobs that may pay little more than the $10.10 minimum wage that went into effect in January 2018. If they are lucky, they may have a part-time job with 20 hours a week or more, which qualifies them for medical coverage.

    Hawaii ranks first in the country in the cost of housing, utilities, transportation and groceries. The median housing value of the state in 2016 was $592,000, making Hawaii the most expensive state in the U.S. to live in. Gasoline is expensive, adding to the costs of commuting long distances from cheaper housing locations. The one positive figure is for health coverage: Hawaii is number two in the nation in terms of the percentage of the population which has health insurance coverage.

● NOTES ●

36 **fall into ...**「…に分かれる、分類される」／46 **ranks first** 1位になっている。／46 **the cost of housing, utilities, transportation and groceries**「住宅、（ガス、水道、電気などの）公共料金、運賃、食料雑貨（代）」／50 **health coverage**「健康をカバーする範囲」health insurance coverage とほぼ同義。

Comprehension Check ▷▶▶▶▶

5. As a place to live, Hawaii ....

   a. is difficult for working families who depend on each adult member working.

   b. has the second highest cost of living in the U.S.

   c. offers one of the best systems of medical treatment.

Structure Practice

A. Choose the one underlined word or phrase that should be corrected or rewritten. Then change it so the sentence is correct.

1. Since Hawaii has ₁ absorbed ₂ succeeding waves of immigrants, there is no single group that can ₃ maintain control over state ₄ politics. [   ]

2. Although some people ₁ used to ₂ look down on the pidgin used in Hawaii, most local people ₃ view it as a way of showing ₄ their identity as local people. [   ]

B. Choose the one word or phrase that best completes the sentence.

3. One thing that .... the Hawaiian Renaissance was a new appreciation of music and chants in the Hawaiian language.

   a. came out of   b. drew from   c. showed up   d. worked into

4. .... with the other states of the country, Hawaii is highly diverse.

   a. In categories   b. In collaboration   c. In comparison   d. In combination

5. Wages available to the working class are .... considering how high the cost of living is.

   a. minimal   b. minimum   c. exceptional   d. exception

Listening Challenge ▶▶▶▶▶

Listen and fill in the missing words.

1. Workers [   ] of Asia to work on the plantations where they cultivated and [   ] and pineapple [   ] Hawaiian sun.

2. With people from so many different countries [   ] languages [   ] that they developed a simple language they [   ] successfully.

3. It is [   ] to learn from residents in Hawaii today that [   ] four different cultures and each spoke a different language.

4. One [   ] it was [   ] the U.S. government to overthrow the Kingdom of Hawaii and [   ] of the island chain.

5. Some people who work in Honolulu [   ] Oahu, leaving home at 5:30 a.m. to get to work by 8:00 [   ] traffic and paying lots of money for gasoline too.

◆ Going Further (for discussion or research)

1. Who was King Kamehameha and what did he achieve?

2. What places in Hawaii do most sightseers want to visit?

CHAPTER 14 連邦政府と州の権利

Federal Government and States' Rights

Differences between federal and state governments

In the early years of American history, the national government played a relatively limited role in the lives of ordinary citizens. The U.S. Constitution left many decisions to the individual state governments. The most contentious issue was whether to allow slavery in a state. Slavery was banned in the North, but allowed in the South. Only after the Civil War was slavery banned in all states by the national government.

Today, some states have laws that prevent minorities, especially blacks, from voting. These minorities have the right to vote, but the state governments make it difficult to exercise that right. Unlike in Japan, residents eligible to vote do not automatically receive a postcard prior to an election. The individual has to go to the local government office and register to vote. Some states require a photo ID in order to register to vote.

If that individual doesn't have a driver's license or a passport, it is difficult to register. Poor people certainly don't have a passport and some don't own a car, so it is difficult for them to prove they are eligible. If the registration office is open only during business hours, the person may have to take a day off—and lose wages—in order to register. This state system makes it difficult for poor and minority citizens to actually vote.

● NOTES ●
1 **national government** ここでは連邦政府のこと。／3 **the individual state governments** 各州政府のこと。／4 **Only after the Civil War was slavery banned … government.**= It was only after the Civil War that slavery was banned … government.／8 **eligible to …**「…する資格がある」／12 **that individual**「その個人」2 行前に言及されている individual のこと。／15 **take a day off**「一日の休暇を取る」

Comprehension Check ▷▷▷▷▷

1. Which statement is true?
   a. Each state has the same basic laws as the other states.
   b. Some states make it difficult for poor people to register to vote.
   c. Slavery was legal in the United States until the twentieth century.

2. How does voter registration in America compare with Japan?

    a. Neither requires a photo ID.

    b. Citizens in both are automatically notified of elections.

    c. Only one requires an actual registration.

🎧 Issue: taxes

41
American citizens and some other residents pay federal income tax and the U.S. Congress makes decisions about how that money is spent. Large percentages of that revenue are used to support the armed forces, federal government bureaucracy, the national pension system, the U.S. Postal Service, and social welfare programs.

The individual states make decisions on their own. A state may want to encourage a company to build a large factory so there will be jobs for its residents. The state government will promise to build new roads to the factory, install a high-quality water supply, and provide a low tax rate to encourage the company to come to that state. The state may also pass "right-to-work laws" that prevent labor unions from organizing in the state. All of these are efforts to bring jobs into the state.

However, there are major downsides to these strategies. Without tax revenues from the company, there will be no budget for local schools, no social welfare funds, and no funding for environmental protection. Paying teachers, maintaining bridges on local roads, putting snowplows on state roads, and even collecting garbage costs the states a lot of money.

● NOTES ●
20 **revenue**「歳入、租税収入」／20 **armed forces**「（全）軍」／21 **the U.S. Postal Service**「アメリカ郵政公社」／26 **right-to-work laws**「労働権法」／31 **snowplow**「除雪機」

Comprehension Check ▷▷▷▷▷

3. Which of the following is not paid for by federal taxes?

    a. American citizens' retirement pensions.

    b. Local roads that do not cross from one state to another.

    c. National military including the army, navy, and air force.

4. State governments are NOT required to pay for which of the following?

    a. Budgets for schools and teaching personnel.

    b. Delivery of mail to individual homes and offices.

    c. Construction and maintenance of local roads.

Issue: textbook adoption

America has no national system of public school textbook adoption. Each state makes its own decisions about which textbooks to use in each grade of elementary, junior high, and senior high school. Some states leave the decision to local school boards in towns and cities, while other states make the decision for the entire state school system.

The content of textbooks is controversial, just as it is in Japan. In progressive states, issues concerning racial and gender minorities are included in the textbooks selected. History textbooks include details about the horrors of slavery and the Holocaust. In conservative states, the focus is on what a wonderful country America is and how everyone has cooperated to build a new nation. History textbooks avoid controversial issues. In states with strong evangelical activist groups, evolution is described as "one theory" together with the Biblical version of Creation. Sex education in those states is virtually nil. Women's rights and Roe v. Wade are not included in the curriculum.

In addition to the gap in textbooks, the gap between states in teacher pay is large. In states with lower tax revenues, some of the worst paid state employees are teachers. Many have to take second jobs even during the school year in order to support their families. This leads to poor education and poorly prepared future employees. This vicious cycle is not easy to break.

● NOTES ●
40 **the Holocaust**「ナチスによるユダヤ人大虐殺」／44 **the Biblical version of Creation**「創世記の聖書訳」／45 **virtually nil**「事実上ゼロ」／45 **Roe v. Wade**「ロー対ウェイド裁判」1973 年、アメリカ連邦最高裁は女性の人工妊娠中絶の権利に合法の判決を下し、人工妊娠中絶を規制するアメリカ国内法の大部分を違憲無効とした。／49 **poorly prepared**「満足な準備が出来ていない」

Comprehension Check ▶▶▶▶▶

5. Which of the following is true?
   a. Selection of textbooks for schools is done within the states.
   b. Textbooks in every state present several controversial issues.
   c. Every state is required to offer courses in sex education.

Structure Practice

A. Choose the one underlined word or phrase that should be corrected or rewritten. Then change it so the sentence is correct.

1. It is ₁standard policy in some states to avoid ₂teach subjects in schools that ₃might offend the religious or political views of ₄students or their parents.

    [   ]

2. I'd like to take ₁a day off in order ₂to finish some business at the city government office but my boss ₃won't make me ₄be away from work for that long.

    [   ]

3. No one ₁in any country seems to ₂enjoy to pay taxes, yet people benefit ₃a lot from social services that ₄are provided by the government.

B. Choose the one word or phrase that best completes the sentence.

4. .... states offer special advantages to companies who are looking for places to build factories, these states might lose out to a competitor.

    a. Unless   b. Without   c. Except   d. Regardless

5. The approval of textbooks in some states is .... by religious activists to include the Biblical view of the Creation of the Universe.

    a. convinced   b. exerted   c. influenced   d. pressurized

82   Chapter 14

Listening Challenge

Listen and fill in the missing words.

1. Publishers of [   ] find it is difficult to produce a [   ] that is liable to be [   ] the whole country.

2. The [   ] of lowering taxes [   ] is that school teachers, [   ], tend to leave states with low pay and move to states [   ] wages.

3. The [   ] in most states is [   ] textbooks to students [   ] and have them return the books [   ] the school year.

4. Some [   ] textbooks for high school students are [   ] in length and [   ] that students don't want to carry them [   ] every day.

5. Each state has a different [   ] requirement for [   ], but most issue a [   ] license to [   ] or over.

◆ Going Further (for discussion or research)

1. Why do some states have a state income tax in addition to federal income tax?

2. What standards do you think should be used in selecting school textbooks?

3. Should the national government—in the U.S. or Japan—choose one textbook for each subject in each year of school?

CHAPTER 15

地域の宗教

Religion in the Regions

🎧 **How important is religion today?**
43
　The original American colonies were founded on belief in religious freedom. That is, each individual should be allowed to practice whatever religion he or she wanted to. The majority of these religions were Christian, either Catholic or Protestant. One cannot help asking how important religion is in America today.

　That does not seem to be the case, according to a Pew Research Center report in 2016. This independent think tank surveyed residents in all 50 states to find out just how "religious" they were, in terms of four simple criteria. They asked residents whether they attended religious worship service at least weekly, prayed at least daily, believed in God with absolute certainty, and held that religion was very important to them.

　The results of the survey showed that five of the six New England states were at the bottom of the list, making New England the "least religious" region in the U.S. Only about 33% of residents in New England described themselves as "highly religious." New England's opposite was the South, where "highly religious" accounted for 60% to 77%. The only outlier was Utah at 64% in the West, which is the center of the Mormon faith.

● NOTES ●
1 **The original American colonies** 第 1 章参照。／5 **That does not seem to be the case**「事実はそうでないようだ」／5 **Pew Research Center**「ピュー・リサーチ・センター」ワシントンに本拠を置く世論調査団体。／7 **criteria**「基準」criterion の複数形。／8 **religious worship service**「宗教的礼拝式」／15 **outlier**「例外値；飛び地」／15 **Utah** [júːtɔː, -tɑː]「ユタ州」／16 **Mormon** [mɔ́ːrmən] **faith**「モルモン教」1830 年アメリカ人ジョゼフ・スミスが始めたキリスト教の一派。

Comprehension Check ▶▶▶▶▶

1. Which statement about religious in America is true?
   a. Religious freedom was a basic belief in the original colonies.
   b. Catholics outnumbered Protestants in the original colonies.
   c. The Protestants were only a small number in the original colonies.

2. The 2016 Pew Research Center survey showed that ....
   a. a majority of people in New England are very religious.

b. people in New England are more religious than those in the South.

   c. the people in the South are more religious than New Englanders.

🎧 Fundamentalists and Evangelicals
44

Commentators on American politics today often point to the significant power of fundamentalists and evangelicals at election time. These are two distinct groups.

Christian fundamentalism is not a single denomination; it is a movement within various denominations. Fundamentalists react against modern culture and liberal ideas. They hold that the Bible is historically accurate and should be taken as literal truth. The Bible says that the world was created in six days and the seventh day is a day of rest. Because the Bible describes Creation one day at a time, they believe each stage was literally one day, and humans were created on a different day from animals. That means that Darwin's idea of evolution is not truth but just "a theory," and it should be taught that way in school textbooks. They believe Mary was a virgin, Jesus was resurrected, the miracles are true events, and Jesus will come again, probably in Jerusalem.

Evangelical Christians believe that Jesus died to save human beings. In order to be saved, an individual must be "born again" in a conversion experience. This experience can be highly emotional and it provides relief at receiving forgiveness from sin. Being born again, a believer will usually participate in missionary work and social activism, including political movements.

● NOTES ●

18 **Fundamentalists**「根本主義者、原理主義者」Fundamentalism「根本主義、原理主義」20 世紀初頭アメリカに起こったプロテスタント教会の教義運動。聖書の記述を文字通りに信じる。／ 18 **Evangelicals**「福音主義者」Evangelicalism「福音主義」キリストの十字架刑による人間の罪の許しを信じ、敬虔な心情と実践を重んじる。／ 20 **denomination**「教派、宗派」／ 23 **Bible describes Creation one day at a time, ...**「聖書は天地創造を一度に一日ずつ説明している、…」聖書によれば、神が天地万物を一日に一つずつ計 6 日間で創造した。／ 30 **be "born again"** be born again「生まれ変わる」／ 30 **a conversion experience**「回心体験」過去の罪や生活を悔い改めて正しい信仰に心を向ける宗教的体験。／ 31 **provides relief at ...**「…で救済になる」

Comprehension Check ▶▶▶▶▶

3. Fundamentalist Christians ....

   a. support liberal social ideas.

   b. belong to different denominations.

   c. do not think the Bible is literally true.

4. People who are Evangelicals do not ....
   a. believe they can be forgiven for their sins.
   b. avoid taking part in mission work.
   c. believe that people have to be "born again."

Who believes what in the West?

A 2018 study of religious beliefs in America shows what residents of the western states believe. Some 64% say they are Christians, and of those, 22% are evangelical Protestants and 23% are Catholics.

Of all adults in the West, only 56% believe absolutely in God, and another 21% are fairly certain that God exists. Regarding attending religious services, 32% go at least once a week, 33% several times a year, and 35% never go.

In terms of where they get guidance on what is right and wrong, adults in the West responded: religion 30%, philosophy 13%, and common sense 44%. When asked about standards for what is right and wrong, 32% said there are clear standards and 65% said it depends on the situation. One of the most interesting statistics in the study regards heaven and hell. While 65% believe that heaven exists, only 50% believe that there is a hell.

When it comes to politics, 50% of adults in the West support smaller government and fewer social services. Some 43% believe that bigger government and more social programs are important. One key issue is abortion. While 39% say that it should be illegal in all or most cases, 57% say it should be legal in all or most cases.

●NOTES●
38 **are fairly certain**「まあまあ確信している」／46 **When it comes to …**「…のことになると」

Comprehension Check ▶▶▶▶▶▶

5. According to the survey, residents of the western states depend mostly on .... when they make decisions about what is right or wrong.
   a. common sense
   b. religion
   c. philosophy

Structure Practice

A. Choose the one underlined word or phrase that should be corrected or rewritten. Then change it so the sentence is correct.

1. While the early Europeans were greatly ₁concern about practicing their religion, it ₂does not seem that ₃present-day residents of New England ₄have the same attitude. [   ]

2. It's not ₁easy grasp exactly ₂what people believe ₃when it comes to religion, and in general it is ₄wise not to ask them. [   ]

B. Choose the one word or phrase that best completes the sentence.

3. People who .... God do so in very different ways.
   a. believe   b. believe in   c. faith   d. faith in

4. An old warehouse was .... a small church building.
   a. converted into   b. reborn for   c. participated in   d. switched on

5. Traditionalists tend to .... against changes in modern life and religious ideas.
   a. react   b. rely   c. reply   d. restore

Listening Challenge ▶▶▶▶▶▶

Listen and fill in the missing words.

1. With [   ], we are [   ] just how often [   ] from London to Oxford.

2. The researchers made [   ] questions they [   ] them learn about people's religious ideas.

3. If you examine [   ], you will discover that most people are not [   ] about whether hell [   ].

4. [   ] a person goes to church, he or she [   ] and relief by reading the Bible [   ] sacred teaching.

5. When [   ] determining the [   ] a tweet, it is important to [   ] original sources.

◆ Going Further (for discussion or research)

1. Do you think that religion is important in the lives of most Japanese people?

2. In what ways does religion affect politics?

Where Are You From?: American Regions
〈地域で見るアメリカ〉

編著者	James M. Vardaman
発行者	山 口 隆 史

発 行 所　　㈱音羽書房鶴見書店

〒113-0033　東京都文京区本郷 3-26-13
TEL 03-3814-0491
FAX 03-3814-9250
URL: http://www.otowatsurumi.com
e-mail: info@otowatsurumi.com

2020年3月1日　　初版発行
2022年3月15日　　2刷発行

組版・装幀　ほんのしろ
印刷・製本　㈱シナノ
■ 落丁・乱丁本はお取り替えいたします。

EC-146